EBUR
HOW TO STOP OVERTHINKING FOREVER

Rithvik Singh is the bestselling author of *I Don't Love You Anymore*, *Thank You for Leaving* and *Warmth*. With a degree in English literature from Hansraj College, University of Delhi, and an unceasing love for writing, he writes to give hope to those looking for it. Formerly a content lead at a storytelling company, Rithvik left his corporate job in 2024 to be a full-time author. With over 5,50,000 followers on Instagram (@wordsofrithvik), his words never fail to feel like home to his readers. Several celebrities have shared his words, including Britney Spears and Huda Kattan, and he has been invited as a speaker to several prestigious institutions across India. Rithvik won the Atta Galatta-Bangalore Literature Festival Book Prize (Popular Choice) and Amazon Popular Choice (Fiction) Award for *I Don't Love You Anymore* in 2024. The book was also shortlisted for the 2024 Kalinga Literary Festival Book Awards (English poetry).

Rithvik lives with his family in Udaipur, but his heart belongs to Delhi. On days when he's missing deadlines, he can be seen struggling (snuggling) with his cat, Cameron, who finds his laptop cosier than any other place in the world for a nap.

How to stop *overthinking* forever

RITHVIK SINGH

EBURY PRESS

An imprint of Penguin Random House

EBURY PRESS

Ebury Press is an imprint of the Penguin Random House group of companies whose addresses can be found at global.penguinrandomhouse.com

Published by Penguin Random House India Pvt. Ltd
4th Floor, Capital Tower 1, MG Road,
Gurugram 122 002, Haryana, India

First published in Ebury Press by Penguin Random House India 2025

Copyright © Rithvik Singh 2025

All rights reserved

10 9 8 7 6 5 4 3 2 1

The views and opinions expressed in this book are the author's own and the facts are as reported by him which have been verified to the extent possible, and the publishers are not in any way liable for the same.

Please note that no part of this book may be used or reproduced in any manner for the purpose of training artificial intelligence technologies or systems.

ISBN 9780143477815

Typeset in Goudy Old Style by Manipal Technologies Limited, Manipal
Printed at Thomson Press India Ltd, New Delhi

This book is sold subject to the condition that it shall not, by way of trade or otherwise, be lent, resold, hired out or otherwise circulated without the publisher's prior consent in any form of binding or cover other than that in which it is published and without a similar condition including this condition being imposed on the subsequent purchaser.

www.penguin.co.in

For my mother—
thank you for never letting
my heart feel heavy.

*I thank my cat, Cameron,
who lives like a prince
and sleeps like a baby.*

CONTENTS

Dear Reader   xi

1. BEST FRIENDS! BEST FRIENDS?   1
2. I'D RATHER TALK ABOUT IT   12
3. UNSOLICITED ADVICE? NO THANK YOU!   22
4. FORTY WAYS TO KEEP YOURSELF BUSY TO AVOID OVERTHINKING   30
5. WHAT'S REALLY IMPORTANT?   40
6. DO YOU *REALLY* LOVE YOURSELF?   47
7. WRITE YOUR HEART OUT   54

CONTENTS

8.	NOTES TO SELF	61
9.	TOXIC THINGS THAT HAVE BEEN NORMALIZED/ROMANTICIZED (BUT THEY SHOULDN'T BE)	69
10.	STAGNANCY OR SELF-LOVE?	87
11.	SELF-LOVE IS (NOT) ENOUGH	97
12.	CAN'T CROSS MY BOUNDARIES	107
13.	OVERTHINKING? OVER IT.	119
14.	EVERYTHING'S FINE, BUT IS IT?	126
15.	CHRONICALLY (ANXIOUS) ONLINE	131
16.	SLEEP ON TIME (CAN'T BELIEVE MOM WAS RIGHT!)	137
17.	SABOTAGE: MADE AT HOME, WITH LOVE	144
18.	RE-PARENTING, BECAUSE WHY NOT?	154

References   163

Dear Reader,

I know you overthink a lot. I know you feel everything too deeply. But I also know that there's immense strength in you. I know you have it in you to build the life of your dreams, one day at a time. In this book, I have tried to include everything I have learned and understood about overthinking.

I hope my words make you feel seen. I hope they make you feel less alone. And above everything, I hope they make you stop overthinking—forever.

I hope this doesn't feel like a book but like a warm hug—a reminder that you're worthy of great things in life. I love you!

Yours,
Rithvik

1

BEST FRIENDS! BEST FRIENDS?

Back in fifth grade, a day before Friendship Day, I remember my mother asking me how many bands I needed but I didn't have an answer. She got me five bands regardless, but I only had one friend.

The next day, I wore four of the bands to school so that everyone thought I had many friends and saved one for the only friend I knew I could give the band to. But when I offered him the friendship band with a smile on my face, he didn't smile back. I realized he didn't have a friendship band for me.

'I'm sorry, I only brought bands for my close friends. Let me see if I have an extra one,' he said. I still remember his landline number; we went in the same school bus together and talked all day long, but he still didn't consider me a friend. It shattered my heart.

In the seventh grade, I made a friend who told me that while we could be friends, we could never be best friends, because he already had one. I thought we were best friends.

When I switched schools in the eighth grade because my mother was transferred to another city, I thought to myself, *this is the fresh start you were looking for. You'll find friends here.* I yearned for friendship with all my heart, but I just couldn't make friends. Although I loved the school and the teachers, and talked to a lot of my classmates, I couldn't find anyone I could truly consider a friend.

In the eleventh standard, I switched schools again, because yet again, my mother had been transferred to another city. This time, I went in with no expectations. But from the very first day, I realized people were warmer and nicer to me. I was still the same person who couldn't make friends, but in that school, people were genuinely interested in talking to me.

My best friend from the same school recently travelled for over 400 kilometres to surprise me at my book signing. Another friend of mine sends me presents every birthday, even though she lives in another country. Another one gives me a handwritten letter every time we meet. I now have friends who check in on me regularly, genuinely care about my success, want me to grow in life and love me wholeheartedly.

The point is, sometimes you cannot find the people who understand your heart, not because you're the problem, but because you're not surrounded by people who are like you. I kept wondering if I was boring or annoying or unworthy of being loved until I found people who made me feel loved without me having to ask them for it. It took me a long time, but I eventually found genuine friends whose sense of humour, mindset and hearts matched me.

I conducted a poll online asking people if they believe their friends secretly dislike them. The results were shocking. Out of the 4811 participants, 3827 (79.5 per cent) believed their friends secretly disliked them. Only 984 (20.5 per cent) participants said 'no'. If you feel insecure in your friendships, this is your reminder that you're not alone. So many of us feel the same way. We feel alone even when we have a lot of 'friends'—mostly because we've not found the right set of people yet.

When a 'friend' refuses to value you, this is what you should replace your thoughts with:

WHAT YOUR ANXIETY MAKES YOU FEEL	WHAT YOU MUST REMIND YOURSELF
I'll never find friends.	The world population is over 8 billion. You'll move to different cities or even countries, switch jobs, meet hundreds of people—you will find your tribe.
Maybe, I'm not doing enough for them.	Give your best. Write it all down—everything you have done for them. Go the extra mile but stop once you realize you're being taken for granted.
I'm unworthy of love.	Make a list of the people who love you. Maybe your parents. Your pet. That teacher who always believed in you. That friend who moved to another city but still manages to stay in touch. You're more loved than your anxiety convinces you to believe.

WHAT YOUR ANXIETY MAKES YOU FEEL	WHAT YOU MUST REMIND YOURSELF
They're not hurting me; I'm just being oversensitive.	Real friends are supposed to understand what triggers you and not judge you for being triggered by the things that make you uncomfortable. You're not oversensitive; they simply do not care about your feelings enough.
I should save the friendship even if it means not telling them how they're making me feel.	Being a good friend to yourself is as important as trying to sustain friendships. You shouldn't hurt yourself by being with someone who doesn't mind seeing you in pain.

If you're someone who constantly overthinks because you do not have friends who feel like home to you, please know that you will find people who will cherish you for who you are and appreciate all your efforts. Just because you have been betrayed by people you thought were your friends in the past doesn't mean you'll be betrayed by everyone you come across in your life.

I was 'friends' with people who didn't return my calls, didn't invite me to hang out with them, didn't believe in my potential, didn't laugh at my jokes and didn't value my efforts. And I realized over time that I didn't lose them. They lost someone who genuinely cared about them. They lost someone who simply wanted a corner in their hearts and was willing to do anything for them in return.

I didn't stop giving my best in friendships because a bunch of ungrateful people don't get to shape my perception of friendships. I knew I wasn't the problem. I knew I'd find people who'd love me for thinking differently from them instead of judging me for it. People who'd understand my jokes and believe in my dreams. People who'd hate to see me hurt. People who'd hold my heart gently on my worst days.

Sadly, what happens when you're giving your best in a friendship and it's not being reciprocated is that you begin to wonder what's missing in you. You see them making efforts for other people and wonder what makes them better than you. But when you start realizing that the feeling of gratitude is rare and that not everyone knows how to value people, you stop getting affected by ungrateful people who couldn't ever value your friendship.

If someone thinks you're not cool enough to be their friend, don't be their friend. If someone thinks you're boring, let them find interesting people. If someone thinks you're too sensitive or too clingy, let them choose someone who isn't. You deserve friends who will love you for who you are and respect your feelings. Friends who know how to be gentle with your heart.

This is what you need to remember if you're yet to find genuine friends:

- Your worth isn't determined by the size of your friend group.
- Your worth isn't determined by the number of people who find you 'interesting'.

- Your worth isn't determined by the number of parties you're invited to.
- Your worth isn't determined by what you do on Saturday nights.
- Your worth isn't determined by how many people sit with you during lunch breaks.
- Your worth isn't determined by the actions of someone who doesn't see the value of your efforts and always takes you for granted.

If you're someone who truly cares about people—you're there for them when they're unwell or upset, you try to make their birthdays special, you try to keep in touch and make plans, you give them advice whenever they ask for it, you believe in their ambitions, you don't say bad things about them behind their back, please know that you deserve friends who do exactly the same for you. And if, despite doing all this for your friends, they're unable to see your worth, letting go of them is a prerequisite for restoring your self-esteem and confidence.

Always remember:

- If someone really cares about you, you will not overthink because of them. They will not make you anxious. They will not drain your energy. They will not make you feel bad about yourself.
- If a friend is making fun of you in front of others, there's a huge possibility that it's not a friend but a secret hater. Friends are supposed to pull each other's leg in private, but yell at the top of their lungs to support their friends in public. You do not have to settle for being the laughing stock just because you're scared of being alone.
- People will suggest that you shouldn't have expectations in friendship. They will talk about low-maintenance friendships, but never forget that there's a difference between low-maintenance friendships and low-quality friendships. Someone can be miles away from you and still manage to support you from a distance, and someone

can be right next to you and still make you feel unwanted.

When you're doing a lot for someone and they make you feel unwanted in return, you keep overthinking what exactly you have done to deserve the cold treatment, the ignorance, the neglect. If nobody has said this to you before, let me say it to you right now: you do not need to overthink because of someone who doesn't care about you. Someone who is determined to ignore everything you do for them. Someone who always chooses other people over you.

You deserve to feel loved, heard, appreciated and understood, and if a friendship doesn't come with that, it's not friendship at all.

2

I'D RATHER TALK ABOUT IT

On my best friend's birthday, I texted her a long paragraph expressing my affection for her—the way my life wouldn't be the same without her and how grateful I was for her presence. A few minutes later, I received a text from her. *Thank You.* Just *Thank You.* No emojis, no emotions, nothing. The moment I saw that text, my brain started convincing me that she was mad at me.

I started wondering what exactly I had done wrong. I started re-reading our conversations from last week, wondering if I had said something unknowingly that she didn't like. A hundred thoughts were fluttering in my head, and that's when I heard the sound of a notification: *my phone was at 1 per cent. While I was typing, it switched off. I'm so grateful to have you in my life. You have made my day! Meet me soon.* I took a deep breath. *Phew.* She wasn't mad at me, her phone had just turned off.

I conducted a poll on my social media handle where I asked my audience what they do when someone hurts them. Out of 4853 participants, only 397 (8.2 per cent) people were okay with confronting the person who has hurt them without overthinking it. On the other hand, 3213 participants (66.2 per cent) revealed that they'd overthink about it for hours, and 1243 participants (25.6 per cent) revealed that they'd first overthink about it and then confront the person. Most people overthink for hours after a conflict instead of simply reaching out to the person and clarifying things.

If the tone of a friend or family member seems off on texts/calls/in person, ask them if

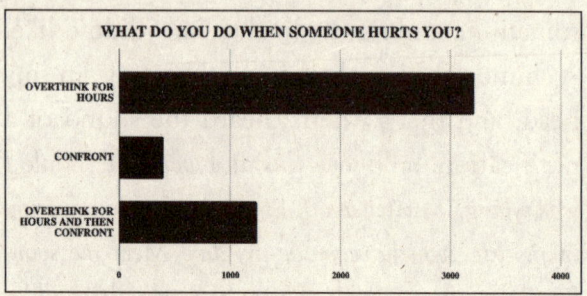

everything's okay. Ask them twice if you're still not convinced. And when they tell you that everything's fine, believe them. Confrontations are better than assumptions. Why are you ruining your mood because you think someone is mad at you? Just ask them if they're upset or mad. Sitting with your thoughts and wondering if someone is mad at you is fruitless.

If the person you're dealing with is not a good communicator or has a hard time expressing their feelings, please know that you cannot coerce someone into telling you something. If you think someone is mad at you but they're not responding clearly—they're neither accepting nor denying, they're brushing it under the carpet, they're pretending like nothing is wrong but their behaviour is suggesting otherwise—please remember that it's not your responsibility to teach people how to talk like adults.

If someone can't come up to you and have a conversation about an issue, and they'd rather live with pent-up frustration and hard feelings, it's their choice. If you have asked someone a couple of times if everything's okay, and if they're still being passive aggressive and nasty instead of just talking about it, take a step back and remind yourself that you don't deserve to stay anxious because of someone who'd rather stay aloof and grow distant than sit, talk and fix things.

Sometimes people take a while to come around. They don't find the right words easily. And that's okay. Give people their space and time. They'll come around and talk about it eventually if they really care about the bond you share. You have done your part, which was reflecting on your behaviour and asking them if anything you said or did had unknowingly offended them.

Certain people expect you to know why they're mad even when you clearly don't. They say things like, *I shouldn't have to tell you why I'm mad. If you love me, you'd know.* While dealing with such people, it's very important not to give in. You cannot read minds. You can introspect and apologize when you know you did something wrong, but you're not responsible for people who expect you to know why they're upset, in a bad mood or in tears before they have even communicated it to you.

One of my closest friends, let's call her Swati, and her boyfriend, let's call him Ankit, had major fights because Ankit would get mad for reasons unknown to Swati, never communicate and expect her to magically know why he was upset because she was dating him.

When you really love someone and care about them, you don't make them overthink by throwing unnecessary tantrums. There's a difference between being genuinely hurt by something that happened and expecting your partner to take responsibility for all your emotions.

When someone tells you, *you love me. I shouldn't have to tell you what's wrong. You should know what's troubling me.* Tell them, *I do love you, and that's why I want to understand what's troubling you. I'm sorry, but I have no idea what this is about. Let's talk about it and find a way to make you feel better?*

When someone says, *I don't want to talk about it,* tell them, *that's alright. Take your time. Just know that I care about you, and when you're ready, I hope we can talk about it.*

You'll have to learn how to stop assuming things and overthinking just because someone doesn't want to communicate their feelings.

INSTEAD OF THINKING THIS	TELL THEM THIS
They're not texting me back on time. Maybe they're not interested in me.	I was wondering why you haven't been texting back on time. I'm not sure if you're busy or need some space. I'd just appreciate some clarity.

INSTEAD OF THINKING THIS	TELL THEM THIS
She hasn't hung out with me in a while. Maybe she doesn't like me any more.	I have been feeling a bit distant lately. Maybe I'm just overthinking, but is everything alright? Let's hangout soon?
They didn't congratulate me/didn't wish me luck before my exam. Maybe I'm the only one who cares.	My friends are my loudest cheerleaders. When you didn't congratulate me, it didn't feel nice. Hope everything's okay between us.
I'm always the one initiating plans. Maybe I'm boring. They don't want to hang out with me.	I always enjoy hanging out with you. But, to be honest, I also want you to make plans. I don't want to feel like I'm the only one pushing for us to meet.
She's making fun of me in front of others and being passive aggressive, but she's telling me nothing's wrong.	I don't appreciate being made fun of in front of others. I'm not the laughing stock. If there's something you'd like to discuss, I'd be happy to, but let's please just talk about it instead of being this way.

While you're busy creating stories in your head, please know that they're merely stories in most cases. You're imagining the worst for no reason. You're feeling sure that terrible things are about to happen, even when they probably won't. Psychologist Albert Ellis called this 'catastrophizing'.

When I was in the tenth standard, I had studied really well for almost all the subjects except math. To say I was terrible at the subject is an understatement. I kept assuming I'd fail. I kept creating scenarios in my head—my friends would make fun of me and my teachers would be disappointed in me. What if I even failed the supplementary exam?

I hadn't gotten the results yet, but in my head, I had failed the math exam as well as the supplementary exam I had to take in case I couldn't pass. The results came, and I hadn't failed. I had scored well in most subjects, and that's when I thought about the number of days I had spent drenched in anxiety for no reason whatsoever. My hypothesis was that I would fail.

But I hadn't left the paper blank. I had attempted a lot of questions. I knew some formulae. I knew some theorems. Sure, I wasn't good at the subject, but assuming I'm going to fail when I had no conclusive reason to think so was my problem.

If you're someone like that—someone who assumes the worst without any reason, know that you're making yourself sad for no reason. Whatever is going to happen is in the future. Why are you making yourself sad about something that hasn't happened yet, or might never actually happen in the future?

When your anxiety tells you that something terrible is going to happen, look at the situation objectively and ask yourself the following questions:

- Am I thinking this because it's definitely going to happen or because I'm scared of it happening?
- Am I letting my fear rise above logic and reason, or am I just being practical?

- Is this a fact or just a feeling?
- If I told a friend I'm thinking this way, and they asked me to justify it, would I be able to, without using my emotions and feelings as a crutch?
- Am I making myself sad by constantly thinking about stuff that isn't in my control?

Stop adding sadness to your life by listening to anxious thoughts instead of believing in yourself, trusting the universe or God or whoever you believe in and knowing that worst-case scenarios shouldn't be the only thing that plays in your head.

You deserve peace, and sometimes choosing your peace means choosing to let go of thoughts that are far from reality.

3

UNSOLICITED ADVICE? NO THANK YOU!

When I was in Class 11, I decided to opt for humanities, but in most Indian households, the subjects a child wants to choose aren't the child's decision. The entire extended family has opinions about what you should do with your life and what stream will be most suitable for you.

The funniest part is that most people giving you career advice are irrelevant—they are unfamiliar with even the basics of what you're aspiring to pursue. They don't know anything about the field. They're not career counsellors. They're far from being an expert on the subject.

But they have opinions. Strong, unflinching opinions. They have this 'I'm-right-and-you're-dumb' attitude. I have no idea where this confidence comes from, but it mostly stems from the space your parents choose to give such people in your life.

The sad part is that your parents are often the ones reaching out to them for advice, not understanding that just because someone's 'successful' doesn't mean they know all the fields. *Mr Verma makes great money. He has a textile business. Let me ask him if you should do law or not.* Statements like these don't make any sense, but our parents sometimes just don't want to look at things practically.

If you need advice, only go to people you really look up to. Don't take advice from people whose interpersonal relationships and finances are messed up. Don't take advice from people who've spent all their lives being stuck in a job they hate.

When you listen to irrelevant opinions and advice, you end up questioning what you originally wanted to do. You begin wondering if what everyone else is saying makes sense and if you're going nowhere with your ideas and plans. But that's not the case.

All my life, I have hated science and math. I barely passed these two subjects and scored the highest in the rest. My parents, however, wanted me to be a doctor, and so, they forced me to study science in the eleventh standard.

When they discussed the possibility of me taking up humanities with my relatives, they said things that have stayed in my head ever since:

He's ruining his life.
He will never have enough money.
Humanities are for those who don't score well.
Your son has scored well. He should take science.

It was only after I started failing all my exams that my parents let me switch to the humanities.

I made it a point to study as hard as I could and do well. I scored 98 per cent in my twelfth boards. I got into Hansraj College, University of Delhi, and you're currently reading one of the many books I have to my name. I have a long, long way to go, but I clearly did not 'ruin my life', and I know I'll always have 'enough money'.

If I had listened to my relatives and not trusted my instincts that told me that I was meant for humanities—for art and literature—I wouldn't be where I am today. You wouldn't have the book in your hands and I'd probably have 'ruined my life'.

Don't miss out on creating your dream life just because some random relative doesn't believe in your potential, ideas and plans.

The problem with most of our relatives is that just because they're older than us, they believe they're naturally smarter. And while they may be smarter than us in the respective fields they have been working in all their lives, to generalize that they always have better ideas and they know better about all aspects of life doesn't make sense to me.

Some of the most problematic, misogynistic, sadistic people I have met are in their fifties and sixties. You can be a terrible decision-maker and a horrible human even when you're old because 'old' and 'wise' are two different things, and they're not synonymous with each other. There are genuinely nice, successful people who give out great advice, but there are also people who aren't nice, aren't successful, are really messed up and give terrible advice with unparalleled confidence. Stay away from them.

You overthink because you involve too many people in your decision-making process. Too many chefs spoil the broth, they say, and it makes perfect sense, because why would you choose to fill your mind with irrelevant advice when you can simply choose to go to either a trained professional or someone who really has built a successful career in the field you're curious to explore.

WHO YOU TAKE ADVICE FROM	WHO YOU SHOULD TAKE ADVICE FROM
Rajesh Uncle who hates his dead-end job.	Career counsellors
Pinky Aunty who doesn't lift a finger to do anything by herself.	Self-made individuals who came from humble backgrounds but worked hard to climb the social ladder.
Suresh Uncle whose son got into a college via a heavy donation.	Teachers from the field you're interested in pursuing.
Ranjit Uncle who is in so much debt, it's concerning.	People who listen to you with an open mind and genuinely want you to grow in life, not just try to prove how they're better than you.

Also, this generation has the gift of AI. You have all sorts of information available at your fingertips.

When you're trying to make a decision, try to use AI to help you:

- Make a pros and cons list. If you're not satisfied, ask it to send you fifty pros and cons. Keep asking for more until you're content.
- Conduct a comparative analysis with your other options. For instance, if you're planning to buy a car, you can just ask AI to make a table comparing two or more cars, their features, market value etc.
- Build step-by-step plans. How can you reach where you want to reach and in how much time— AI can tell you everything.
- Ask all the 'what if' questions, including but not limited to, what if this doesn't work out? What if my relatives are right? (Tell AI what exactly they're saying, and it'll tell you objectively if they're making sense or not.) What if I regret this? What should be the next step? So on and so forth.

Please don't get confused and anxious because of people who don't care if you do well in life or not, but only care about refuting your ideas and beliefs to make the point that they're older and wiser, and you're a child who doesn't know what's good or bad for you.

The people who truly care about you want you to grow in life and be happy, with or without abiding by a plan that they approve of. They will celebrate you right from day one—they will cheer so loudly for you that your faith in yourself will grow, too.

4

FORTY WAYS TO KEEP YOURSELF BUSY TO AVOID OVERTHINKING

1. Discover new music. Your playlist may have a lot of songs, but there are a lot of gems you haven't discovered yet. Listen to new artists. Explore new genres. Or just blast music in your bedroom and dance your heart out.
2. Create a scrapbook of your favourite memories. Include pictures of all your favourite people and places. Whenever you revisit the scrapbook, a sense of gratitude will kick in, and you'll feel better.

3. Journal your happy memories. Write about the time you went on a vacation, or when your best friend made you feel special, or when you scored well or won a competition. Write it all down so that when your anxiety tells you that your life isn't beautiful, the journal tells you otherwise.
4. Go to a park in the morning or evening and take a walk. Chances are, you'll find a lot of older couples doing laughter therapy, yoga or just walking. Take a long walk in the park with your favourite music playing in your earphones. When you move your body, you slowly take yourself out of the overthinking zone.
5. Rewatch episodes of an old favourite show or a movie that you haven't watched in a while. Something you are already familiar with. Something that brings you comfort and joy. To me, *Modern Family*, *New Girl* and *Schitt's Creek* really bring happiness and help reduce overthinking.

6. Call someone. Reconnect with someone you haven't talked to in a while or just call your best friend. Call someone from your family you love. Have a long conversation with someone.
7. Make videos of yourself. Reels. Trends. You don't have to post them. Just make fun videos by yourself or with your friends to stay distracted.
8. Try learning how to cook a new recipe or order your comfort food. Cooking can be extremely helpful because it requires all your attention. Watch a YouTube tutorial and get going.
9. Write a letter to your inner child. I write one to mine every month. Write about everything you did in the past month—apologize to yourself for every time you weren't kind to yourself and remind yourself that you do not deserve hostility, but soft love.
10. Play a board game. With friends or alone—online. When we were young, all my cousins

would sit together and play Ludo. Hands down, one of the best bonding exercises ever.
11. Read a book. It doesn't necessarily have to be a complicated one. Visit a library/bookstore, and if you find it difficult to focus on reading, pick up any thin book with a big font. When the book isn't very lengthy, your motivation to read it is less likely to die.
12. Consume wholesome content—cat or dog videos, inspiring talks, travel vlogs, stand-up comedies, painting or calligraphy process videos, DIY videos etc.
13. If you're lucky enough to be in touch with your grandparents, sit with them and ask them to tell you stories from their childhood. The stories will stay with you forever. Do the same with your parents.
14. React to all the memes your friends have sent you. Or the messages you haven't opened yet. Text someone you haven't heard from in a while.

15. Take out your dusty childhood album from your cupboard and revisit those memories—the way you were carefree and happy. A reminder that life can't always hurt you.
16. Learn a new language. Who knows when life will take you to Paris? You should be prepared. It'll also give you a sense of achievement.
17. Workout. And when I say workout, I don't mean heavy weight training. Do it, if it works for you, but what I mean by workout is moving your body. Pilates. Zumba. Dancing. Jogging. Playing a sport. Do whatever works for you the best. Do what you really enjoy. Showing up for your physical health is important.
18. Take a trip to where you have always wanted to go. And if you can't travel, explore your own city like a tourist. Visit your comfort places in the city you live in.
19. Scroll through Pinterest and print out positive affirmations or quotes, or just photographs that inspire you and make you

feel better. Paste them somewhere you can see them every day.

20. Look for pictures you have always wanted to post but forgot to or never had the time to. Post them all.
21. Take your parents or loved ones out. A nice family dinner. A weekend getaway. Or cook for the people you love and invite them over. Anything works.
22. Learn about things you're curious about. For instance, I love learning new words. I love learning new things about horticulture. I love reading lesser-known facts about authors. Watch videos. Read articles. Satiate your curiosity.
23. Grab your cozy blanket. Set the AC temperature to whatever is ideal for you, and take a long afternoon nap. A good sleep can be extremely helpful.
24. Clean your room. When you clean your room or rearrange your wardrobe, it'll provide your mind with a sense of control—you will feel better and calmer.

25. To quote George Eliot, 'What do we live for, if it is not to make life less difficult for each other?' Visit an old-age home or an NGO. Do something good for others and your heart will definitely feel better.
26. Wear your favourite outfit. Buy yourself flowers. Every time I organize a book signing, I give out flowers to whoever attends. A lot of men tell me that they have never received flowers. You need to allow yourself to be loved fully—by yourself and by others.
27. Write letters to your loved ones. Take a beautiful piece of paper, express how much you appreciate someone's presence and give it to them when you meet them. Letters are heartfelt, and we need to bring them back.
28. Take a long shower. Shampoo your hair. Play your favourite music in the background.
29. Work on your skin. Explore sheet masks and serums. Try home-made remedies. Your skin deserves to glow.
30. Print out Polaroids of your favourite memories and put them up in your room—a

reminder that happiness had found you before, and so, it'll find you again soon. Frame them with fairy lights for an added artistic touch.

31. Join a new course/class. My best friend is a psychologist, and she took a flower arrangement class recently. I once took an online course on calligraphy. Enrol yourself in anything that interests you, it doesn't matter if it's linked to your career or not. The intent is to ensure you feel better.

32. Buy yourself a plant. The joy of watching a rose bloom after you have spent days taking care of the plant is unparalleled. Be a plant parent.

33. Play with your aesthetic. Are there any specific shirts you saw on Pinterest but haven't tried styling yet? Is there a jewellery piece you want to experiment with? Scroll through Pinterest and reinvent yourself.

34. Play with your pet or with your friends' pets. I spend at least an hour every day with my cat, Cameron, and that is undoubtedly one

of the best parts of my day. Get a pet, if possible (only if you can really take care of them). Having a pet is really good for your mental health.

35. Plan your week—note down everything you look forward to doing. Once everything's on paper, the vision is clear, and it's harder to procrastinate.
36. Discard the things you're holding on to that only hurt you—photographs of exes, the presents they gave you, the cards they made you etc. Why would you hold on to things that don't put a smile on your face but make your heart heavy?
37. Open the windows of your room. Keep the lights on. Don't sit in the darkness. You make yourself sadder by sitting in the dark and listening to sad music when you need to sit in the sun and soak in the light.
38. Mediate, but only if it works for you. Whenever I try to meditate, it only makes me more anxious. Listening to peaceful

ASMR or songs, spending quality time with the ones you love, sitting under a tree and letting the wind touch you—I believe they serve the same purpose.
39. Find out more ways to make money. Plan a business. Invest. Watch YouTube videos. Get a side job. The more money you make, the easier most things in your life will be.
40. Remind yourself that everything your heart deserves will find you soon. Pain can't be your destination; you're destined for miracles, boundless love and blessings.

5

WHAT'S REALLY IMPORTANT?

There are two types of people in this world—the ones who let anxiety take over them and paralyse them, and the ones who choose to focus on what's in their control and find solutions to the problems they're encountering.

For instance, two people, Person 1 and Person 2, have a math exam tomorrow.

Person 1 is lying in bed, staring at the ceiling, thinking about everything likely to go wrong.

What if I forget all the formulae?
What if I leave the answer sheet blank?

> *What if the paper is so difficult that I end up failing?*
> *What if most of the questions are from the units I have not studied properly?*

Person 2 is worried about the exam but knows that they cannot afford to lie in bed and overthink. He knows that he has zero control over things like:

> *Whether or not his memory will support him.*
> *Whether or not the paper will be difficult.*
> *Which units the questions will come from.*

He knows what he can control is how prepared he is. Person 1 has lost sight of what's really important because they're letting their thoughts run amok. He is not forcing himself to get out of bed despite knowing he has an exam tomorrow. Chances are, because he is lying in bed overthinking, he is missing out on learning important formulae or revising important topics.

Shakespeare once wrote, 'Things without all remedy / Should be without regard. What's done is done.' Worrying about something before it has happened and after it has happened has no consequence. When you focus on the things that are in your control, you save yourself from future anxiety. You save yourself from making things worse.

I was once friends with someone—let's call him Arhaan—who would keep telling me how worried he was because he hadn't studied properly. A week before every exam, he'd start ranting: *I have not studied anything. I'm so worried. What if I fail? What if the paper is really difficult?* But you know what he'd do all week? Party with his friends. Spend hours playing football. Skip school and be chronically online. After a point, I stopped sympathizing with his anxiety. He was choosing not to do anything about what was making him anxious. Ranting about it had become a defence mechanism for him. He didn't care to find a solution, and so, he never found one.

WHAT'S REALLY IMPORTANT?

When I was young, I used to keep worrying about my dog, Roxy, passing away. I was worried about that ever since he was a month old. I spent days and weeks wondering how I'd spend my life without him, when he was still very much there in my life. I was so scared of losing him that I spent years stressed out about everything. *What if he falls sick? How will I survive without him? How will I watch his body?* All while he was completely fit, happy and healthy. He lived a full life and died a peaceful death. I spent over ten years worrying about his demise and now, when I look back, I feel so sad for my younger self because nobody deserves to live with so much anxiety. Why was I anxious about something that didn't happen for another ten years? Instead of being grateful to have been loved by a dog so unconditionally, I was worried about losing him. All. The. Time. I was creating my own pain by creating scenarios that made me miss out on so many moments when I could've just been happy—if only I wasn't busy overthinking about what might go wrong.

When you spend your time overthinking something, you create worst-case scenarios in your mind and hurt yourself unnecessarily. When you repeat a scenario in your mind, the fear of the scenario turning into reality increases, and you keep expecting the worst. It's a vicious loop.

The key is to focus on what's in your control.

For instance, if you're stressed out about a job interview, it's in your control to show up on time, be well-prepared, answer politely, watch/read a lot of interview tips and tricks online, carefully read the job description and requirements etc. What's not in your control is whether or not they'll like you, if the others will be more prepared than you or not, if it'll be a nice company to work at or not etc.

When you focus on the latter, you ruin what's in your control because you unknowingly end up wasting a lot of time and energy on the inconsequential. Instead of making yourself sad by letting your mind convince you that everything is going to fall apart, do what's required of you to ensure you're confident.

A technique used in Cognitive Behavioural Therapy (CBT) called 'Worry Time' has been really helpful for me to stop overthinking unnecessarily. It advises you to allocate a specific time in a day to think about the source of your anxiety and try to find solutions—whatever you're worried about. This ensures you don't spend the entire day worrying and overthinking. This way, you get to think about what's making you anxious and also find solutions to it, but all within the stipulated fifteen to twenty minutes you have allocated to the same. The rest of the day, whenever you feel like thinking about the problem, remind yourself that you will think about it, just not in that moment. There's a time for the same, and you must consciously refuse to let it take more space than it deserves.

Worrying is a sign that you care about something, but sitting around and not working for something is a sign that you care more about the things that might go wrong than the things that you possess the power to ensure go right. Claim your power back. Your anxiety shouldn't be allowed to make you stuck. You need to move your mind to the right position by prioritizing and focusing on the right thoughts and proceeding with the right actions that will be good for your growth and mental peace. To quote psychologist Viktor Frankl, 'Between stimulus and response, there is a space. In that space is our power to choose our response.'

When you're lying on the couch and overthinking, remind yourself that you don't deserve to hurt yourself like that. You deserve kindness, and it begins with not letting negative thoughts take over your being.

You can't control everything, but you can always choose to focus and work on what is really in your control.

6

DO YOU *REALLY* LOVE YOURSELF?

If you respect your body, you wouldn't consume junk food every day. You wouldn't let your sugar levels rise. You wouldn't skip exercising.

If you respect your mind, you wouldn't fill it with thoughts that make you sad. You wouldn't allow unpleasant thoughts to build a home inside your head because you genuinely care about your well-being.

Anybody who truly loves and respects themselves will not sit around for hours overthinking random situations. Think of your mind as your child. Would you nurture your child with love, hope and care? Or will you ensure the child always stays restless and anxious by wrapping them in a blanket of unpleasant and irrational thoughts?

Self-love and chronic overthinking cannot coexist. You cannot claim to love and respect yourself while torturing yourself every day by thinking about the worst-case scenarios all the time.

When you love yourself, protecting your peace becomes a priority. You don't engage in things that aren't good for you—overthinking, for instance.

OVERTHINKER	SELF-LOVING PERSON
Obsesses over his flaws.	• Knows he's worthy of love. • Truly believes he has what it takes to be the best version of himself, and strives to improve himself every single day.

OVERTHINKER	SELF-LOVING PERSON
Over analyses every statement, compliment or comment.	• Doesn't think twice before confronting someone if they say something sarcastic/hurtful. • Talks about his feelings openly. • Respects himself enough to know that he deserves all the applause and praise.
Fears vulnerability and keeps pushing people away because they thinks they're easy to replace.	• Allows himself to be loved by people and loves with an open heart. • Doesn't equate his worth with someone's inability to love him.
Thinks people are doing him a favour by staying in his life. Tolerates toxic people because he's scared of being alone.	• Believes that it's an honour to be a part of his life. • Appreciates everything he brings to the table. • Knows that even if someone leaves him, that's not the end of the world. • Believes that his goodness and personality will always connect him with the right people.

OVERTHINKER	SELF-LOVING PERSON
Keeps trying to fix/change himself for others.	• Takes suggestions and advice but doesn't keep trying to please people unnecessarily. • Remains kind to everyone, including himself and when the kindness isn't reciprocated, leaves. • Doesn't pretend to enjoy things he truly doesn't enjoy only to fit in. • Doesn't put up with problematic behaviour or justify toxicity.
Can't stop thinking about the past.	• Has his share of regrets and stories of pain, but doesn't let it become a force that shapes his identity or dictates the course of his life. • Doesn't go back to the people who've hurt him. • Doesn't forgive easily. • Knows he can create a beautiful life for himself and focuses on that instead of living in a past that has long died.

OVERTHINKER	SELF-LOVING PERSON
Over explains and over apologizes.	• Doesn't apologize when he hasn't made a mistake only to please someone or convince them to stay in his life. • Would rather say goodbye to someone than beg them to stay in his life. • Knows when to let go when someone hurts him. • Doesn't over explain his feelings repeatedly to someone who's determined to misunderstand him.
Always feels guilty for setting boundaries.	• Doesn't ever compromise with his boundaries. • If someone cannot respect him, he cannot keep them in his life. • Keeps his self-respect on a pedestal, always.

OVERTHINKER	SELF-LOVING PERSON
Is always scared of rejection.	• Knows that he cannot win every time and that's okay because his worth isn't determined by how often he wins or loses. • His worth is determined by his perseverance, his ability to keep moving forward and knowing that a failed job interview doesn't equate to a failed career. Just because an interviewer didn't like him doesn't mean no other interviewer will either. • Trusts his hard work and talent enough to not undermine himself.
Stays quiet because of the fear of judgement.	• Voices his opinions confidently and accepts and apologizes when he unknowingly ends up saying something wrong. • Doesn't hide himself in the background. • Values his thoughts, ideas and beliefs without needing someone else to validate them for him.

If you truly love yourself, you will keep trying not to get lost in your head. Loving yourself is about creating a safe space for your mind where anxiety can be an occasional guest but never a permanent resident, and you know how and when to ask it to leave. It's about choosing your peace and well-being every day, and the very fact that you picked up this book is a sign of self-love—that you genuinely want to stop overthinking.

7

WRITE YOUR HEART OUT

Almost everyone has, at some point in their life, been recommended to journal. By an article or a video. A friend or a therapist. But so few of us really try journaling. Mostly because we don't understand the impact it has.

When you talk to a friend or a family member, you keep certain things to yourself because of the fear of judgement. There are very few people whom you can really pour your heart out to, and even to them, there are parts of your heart that will always remain alien.

Think of it this way—your journal is your best friend, but no social norms are stopping you from venting in it. You can rant in any language you want to, in any form or structure—it's your safe space to let it all out without the fear of judgement.

When you put the thoughts that are swirling around in your head on paper, your heart feels lighter. You feel less alone. When I was in college, I fell in love with someone who didn't love me back. I wasted months overthinking why that person couldn't just love me back. My grades and self-esteem started dropping. That's when journaling changed everything for me.

I started writing letters to her in my journal. Letters I would never send to her. When I'd write things like, *why can't you love me? Will anyone ever love me? Why did you make me feel like I meant something to you when I clearly didn't?* I realized that I was functioning in a pathetic state. While writing those letters, it hit me—I was repeatedly begging someone to love me, and while she went on with her life normally,

I was messing up my schedule, my grades and my mental health. I tore off all the letters and started writing about the reasons why I loved her. I realized she hadn't done a lot for me. She had just been a friend. I, on the other hand, was doing a lot for her, perhaps in the hope of dating her eventually.

The moment I wrote down the things I had done for her and compared them to everything she did for me, my eyes opened. I made a list of everything hurtful she had said to me. I recalled all the incidents when I cried because of her, how I felt when my grades dropped, how I felt when I saw her with another guy—I wrote it all down. And somewhere in the process of documenting my reality, I found my self-respect back.

I wrote everything in the. third person. Let's call the girl Shreya. For instance, Rithvik brought Shreya chocolates, but she ended up giving them to one of her friends. Shreya knew Rithvik wasn't doing well, but she didn't even check in on him to ask if he was okay.

I came across a research paper by Dr Ethan Kross and Dr Özlem Ayduk where they talk about the idea of 'self-distancing'—how you can mentally step back and observe your situation from a third-person point of view to make sense of your feelings. When you become an observer instead of a feeler for a moment, you look at things more objectively and stop your thoughts from going haywire.

Things to remember while journaling to stop overthinking:

1. Grammar and sentence structure do not matter. Only your feelings do.
2. It's okay if there's no chain of thought you're following. Set a timer for half an hour and don't stop writing. Write down everything that comes to your mind. I learned about this while doing my undergrad in literature. In literature, this is called 'stream of consciousness' an unorganized free flow of thoughts.

3. Don't judge yourself for having written how you truly feel. Acknowledgement of feelings precedes the reasoning of feelings.
4. Your journal doesn't have to look aesthetically pleasing for it to be a valuable tool in your journey. Not everything has to be social media-friendly. Feelings are messy. Our lives are messy. It's okay.
5. Don't interrupt your thoughts because you're scared of facing them. Let it all come to you, and when it does, let it all out on paper.
6. You don't always have to journal to find a solution. If you just want to rant, that's completely okay. You don't have to judge yourself for it.
7. If a thought comes to you more than once, write it down as many times as it comes. It's demanding your attention.
8. When you write about your lowest moments in your journal, I want you to tear off the pages once you're done writing them, or else you'll keep going back to them. You don't

need to hold on to what hurts you and feel the same pain repeatedly.
9. It's okay to draw, make lists or doodle how you feel if words fail you. The point is to let it all out, raw and unfiltered.
10. Be true to your feelings. Write how you *really* feel, not how you intend the world to perceive how you feel. Nobody's going to read your journal. Be honest in it.

When you're overthinking, your anxiety makes you question everything you have done in life. You begin questioning your worth and start feeling bad about yourself. This used to happen with me as well. Documenting my gratitude has really helped me feel better on days when my overthinking tries to convince me that my life sucks. Whenever I have a really happy day, I write about it in my journal. I call that journal 'My Happy Place'. When I got into my dream college, I wrote down about how my mother had tears of joy in her eyes, how she hugged me and we celebrated. I wrote down the names of everyone who congratulated me. The way my best friend sent me flowers. Everything. That day has passed, but it still remains documented in 'My Happy Place' so I can come back to it whenever I feel low.

Something I really want to start practising now is documenting my gratitude daily. Not just the grand moments, but also the small moments of joy in my everyday life. Having a really scrumptious pastry, watching the rain from my window, discovering a new song that put a smile on my face, talking to a friend after a long time, finding a shirt I thought I had lost etc. It's easy to forget small things that make you happy because they don't cause monumental shifts in your life. But that doesn't make them unimportant. They're always worth celebrating.

Consider the thousands of thoughts in your head, butterflies and your journal, the garden where you release them. For your peace, let them flutter in there instead of your mind.

8

NOTES TO SELF

Simply put, affirmations are thoughts you consciously plant in your head. You choose a thought and keep repeating it. Now, you may or may not believe in the power of affirmations, but you must understand that there's no harm in feeding your mind with good thoughts. When you're overthinking, you absent-mindedly think about the worst-case scenarios. When you choose to remind yourself of positive affirmations and make them a part of your life, the way you perceive situations and yourself changes. It's not about whether they work or not—it's about choosing to remind yourself how you truly deserve to feel, even in moments when you're not feeling that way.

Sometimes, you need to make promises to yourself. With self-love comes the responsibility of moving away from thoughts, people and situations that make you feel bad about yourself and negatively affect your self-esteem. When you remind yourself of the promises you're supposed to keep and the affirmations you need to remember at all times, you build a life where peace always remains your priority, and it's never compromised.

When I talk about affirmations and promises to make to yourself, I in no way imply that you're not allowed to feel sad or break down on certain days. You're only human, and you will have your share of days that will leave you restless and anxious. When I talk about affirmations and promises, it's so that even on those days, you can remind yourself that no matter how you're feeling in that moment, you deserve better. It's about ensuring you let go of the pain once you have felt it. It's about not staying stuck in the past.

And more than anything, affirmations and promises are reminders that self-love doesn't leave when anxiety enters—the former ensures the latter doesn't overstay. The intent isn't to pretend and gaslight yourself into believing everything is okay—it's to ensure you believe in yourself enough to know that you have the strength to feel better over time and make the right decisions for yourself, without letting anxious feelings and thoughts take over you.

Here are forty affirmations/promises that will help you calm yourself down when you're overthinking:

1. The universe (or God) loves me unconditionally and is always looking after me.
2. Good things will always find me because I deserve them.
3. My mind is my happy place, and I'm willing to do everything it takes to ensure that.

4. My inner child deserves to feel safe, and I will ensure that I'm always trying to ensure that.
5. I'm always protected, safe and loved.
6. I love myself, and that's why I don't listen to my anxious thoughts.
7. My heart deserves consistent tenderness.
8. I gently return my focus to what's truly important—my peace, growth and my loved ones.
9. I'm allowed to slow down. I deserve to slow down.
10. Overthinking is in my control. I'll not let my anxiety convince me otherwise.
11. I refuse to make myself sad about things that aren't in my control.
12. My worth isn't determined by the opinions of the people around me.
13. I deserve love that comes with peace—uncomplicated, simple, persistent love.
14. I don't have to over analyse every situation or statements made by others or myself.
15. I'm powerful enough to bring myself out of the overthinking loop.

16. I have it in me to stay calm even when my anxiety wants me to panic. Especially when my anxiety wants me to panic.
17. Not every thought deserves my attention.
18. Not every thought makes sense, and that's okay.
19. There's self-love in pausing.
20. There's peace in not over analysing trivial matters.
21. When my friends aren't doing well, I take care of them. And so, when I'm not okay, I will not forget that I'm a friend to my heart, too. I will choose to be kind to myself.
22. I do not live in the past, and I don't allow the past to control how I live.
23. Revisiting toxic thoughts and replaying bad experiences isn't something self-loving people do. I refuse to make myself sad about situations that I have already lived and dealt with. I choose to move past my past.
24. My anxiety is a liar. I don't make friends with liars.

25. My future is full of amazing people and opportunities.
26. I'm strong enough to say goodbye to deprecating thoughts.
27. I choose to release my negative thoughts because even if I cannot stop them from entering my mind, I have the power to decide how long they stay.
28. I'm patient with my heart.
29. Life has its magical ways of ensuring peace finds me, and it stays.
30. I have the strength to never surrender to my thoughts.
31. I'm choosing calm, for myself and the people who matter to me.
32. Happy thoughts keep blooming in my mind.
33. My self-esteem, self-care and self-love will always be precious to me. They are my topmost priorities.
34. Finding solutions is important, but not at the expense of my mental health. Never at the expense of my mental health.

35. It's not my responsibility to overthink because of people who are careless with their words and actions.
36. I do not owe my attention to anything that doesn't take me closer to becoming the person I have always wanted to be.
37. I'm allowed to walk away from irrational thoughts and feelings that are here to hurt me.
38. I'm always grateful for the people who love me, especially for myself.
39. All the answers aren't mine to find.
40. Just like everything else, this, too, shall pass.

Please remember that it doesn't matter whether you start your day with affirmations, end your day with them, or practice them in the middle during your lunch break at work. What truly matters is that you make them a part of your day.

In addition to these affirmations, what might help you is the 'Self Affirmation Theory' developed by social psychologist Dr Claude Steele in 1988. In its essence, it talks about how in the face of failure, we feel terrible about ourselves, and we can feel better about ourselves by reminding ourselves about our qualities and achievements, independent of what has gone wrong. For instance, when you fail an exam, it's hard not to question your worth. But when you remind yourself about your other qualities—you're a kind person, you're good at sports, you know how to play the guitar etc., you feel better because you somehow remind yourself that this failure alone doesn't define you. You have qualities worth cherishing. Your worth isn't determined by a single event where things didn't work out the way you wanted them to.

9

TOXIC THINGS THAT HAVE BEEN NORMALIZED/ROMANTICIZED (BUT THEY SHOULDN'T BE)

1. ONE-SIDED LOVE

There are hundreds of songs romanticizing loving someone who doesn't love you back. Tens of movies about the same subject. When I was young, I too wrote extensively about the feeling of being in love with someone who doesn't love you back. Here's the problem with romanticizing one-sided love:

- Movies and songs indicate that if you love someone with your whole heart, even if they don't love you back, you must continue loving them and holding on to those feelings without moving on. It's implied that true love lies in holding on to those feelings even when it hurts. But when you continue to keep hoping someone will love you back, you end up overthinking for weeks and months, if not years. You begin to overthink why they don't love you back. You start equating your worth with their lack of reciprocation. It's extremely toxic and has terrible repercussions for your mental health.
- Nobody talks about how unfair it is to keep chasing someone who doesn't feel the same way about you. One-sided lovers often overstep boundaries because they want to win the person over by giving them what they don't want. The inability to accept rejection often leads to invasion of boundaries, stalking and obsessive behaviour.

- Movies, songs and books don't talk about accepting rejection gracefully instead of taking it personally. When you realize that someone doesn't feel the same way about you, the best thing you can do is walk away from them—to save your self-respect and also respect the other person's feelings. Waiting endlessly for someone to love you back is a form of self-harm.
- Just because someone doesn't feel the same way about you doesn't make them a villain. You'll find someone who will love you so much that you'll wonder why you wasted so many years of your life chasing after the people who didn't care about you.
- Instead of overthinking why someone doesn't love you back, instead of trying to find flaws in yourself and fixate on them, try to look at it this way: you can't plant feelings in someone's heart just because they exist in yours. And that doesn't mean you're unworthy of love. It simply means

that you're feeling too much for someone who doesn't feel as much for you—and that's okay. You will get over it eventually and be happy again. There was a time when you didn't know them and you were happy, and you will be happy again.

2. BRUTAL HONESTY

The people who comment on your appearance/career choices/family background because they're 'real' and 'brutally honest' are just bullies you need to get rid of. Here's the problem with 'brutal honesty':

- Empathy is the bare minimum. If someone cannot be kind and considerate, they don't deserve you.
- There are always gentler ways of expressing things. You don't need to hurt someone to familiarize them with the 'truth'. To quote Maya Angelou, 'I have learned that people will forget what you said, people will forget

what you did, but people will never forget how you made them feel.'
- Brutal honesty creates a gulf between you and the other person. As Arundhati Roy said, 'That's what careless words do. They make people love you a little less.'
- There's beauty in being compassionate when you're trying to help someone. Your intentions don't matter as much as your actions do. Your heart can be in the right place, but please make sure your words are a reflection of the same.
- It's important to call your friends out when they're making terrible life decisions or when you're concerned about their well-being, but your concern should feel like concern, not disrespect or mockery. Your words can make someone overthink for weeks.

3. BEING RUDE ONLINE

- We've normalized trolling people in the comments. We find it funny to dehumanize someone just because there are no legal or tangible repercussions. People creating content constantly feel unsafe because of the ruthless trolling they go through. Their self-image is impacted terribly, and the people who troll them aren't held accountable. What happens when we normalize trolling people online is that we're normalizing being insensitive in general. When you make fun of someone for their accent, you end up making a lot more people insecure about their accents—the people who sound like them and are reading your hurtful comments. When you make racist comments, you make an entire community feel unsafe. When you comment on someone's physical appearance, know that a lot of people share similar physical attributes, and you're triggering all of them.

- All the people in my life who use dating apps have talked to me at some point or the other about people being rude to them on those platforms. When my friend refused to meet a guy, he sent her a really abusive voice note, followed by a threat, and she immediately deleted all the dating apps because she didn't feel safe any more. There needs to be stricter laws against cyberbullying. People assume that the person they're abusing, mocking or bullying doesn't have feelings just because they can't see that person in real life. That's not the case. People overthink for months over incidents that happen to them online.

- It's important to know that you're allowed to block and report people who trigger your overthinking in online spaces. You must report instances of bullying to the cyber cell. You must not let disrespectful behaviour slide.
- Manners, respect and basic empathy aren't optional—both offline and online.
- You don't need to overthink because of an anonymous person on the Internet who goes around spreading hate. Insecure people try to feel better about themselves by pulling others down. They carry a lot of unresolved emotional pain within themselves. Secure people never hate. Healed people never hate.

4. THE IDEA THAT RESPECT CAN BE ONE-SIDED

My relatives would insult me and my parents, and I'd not retaliate. Neither would my parents. Their hurtful words would keep echoing in my ears for days and weeks. I'd lose sleep and feel extremely anxious. I'd feel terrible about myself because they'd say horrible things about me, and I was too young to understand that whatever they said wasn't facts. Please note that:

- Nobody is allowed to make you feel bad about yourself, no matter their age.
- It doesn't make you a bad person to take a stand for yourself and your parents against a bully whom you're advised to respect just because they're related to you.
- The people who love you won't hurt you, and you don't owe any love or respect to the people who keep hurting you.
- If a relationship requires you to turn into a doormat, it's better to sweep the relationship out of your life instead.

- Respect is earned, and not everyone deserves it.

5. SELF-BLAMING

Whenever something would go wrong, my grandmother would say, 'I must've done terrible things in my past life. That's why all this is happening to us.' When my father didn't get promoted three years in a row, he said, 'I think God is angry with us.'

Here's what you need to understand:

- When someone blames their past life for their current hardships, it makes them feel responsible (in a way) for things that they might have no control over. You mustn't blame yourself for things that aren't in your control.
- Sometimes things don't work out, and that doesn't mean God (if you believe in the idea of God) isn't working in your favour. If there's a higher power, it's compassionate and kind. It only wishes you well.

- Not every hardship is 'deserved'. Sometimes life is unfair, and you don't need to convince yourself otherwise.
- Sometimes you work hard and give your best, but things don't work out, and that's okay. You don't need to be so hard on yourself unnecessarily.

6. NOT SPENDING MONEY ON YOURSELF

My mother taught me something that I couldn't be more grateful for—spending money on myself without thinking twice. She taught me the following:

- If you make Rs 1,00,000, spend at least Rs 30,000 on what you truly love. It doesn't have to make sense to anybody. Buy anything you want. Don't let your needs and responsibilities be your entire life.
- You'll never feel motivated to go to work if you're not spending money on yourself.

- Saving for the future is important, but not every purchase has to be an investment, and not every penny needs to be saved.

7. HAVING A TOXIC JOB

I have not met many people who love their jobs. Almost everyone hates their manager. Almost everyone has a few toxic people at their workplace who don't respect others, overburden employees and don't care about their mental health. This is what you need to remember:

- Just because the people in your family spent twenty years working a job they didn't like doesn't mean you're obligated to follow the same trajectory.
- It's wise to save money for a few months and look for better job opportunities than staying in a toxic work environment.
- You don't need to tolerate disrespect from a sadistic manager who doesn't understand how kindness works.

- You don't need to feel guilty about setting boundaries at work.
- You're not obligated to show up on the weekends.
- Your talent defines you, not the perception of your seniors at work determined to belittle you.
- 'Everyone hates their job' is not an excuse for you to stay at a place that's terrible for your mental health.
- You don't need to overthink because of someone who cannot value your efforts. What's not enough for your current company will be celebrated by other companies.
- Don't be scared of leaving. You landed this job, you're capable of getting another one. A better one, in fact.

8. NOT HAVING REAL CONVERSATIONS

When was the last time you called your best friend and had a heart-to-heart with them?

We're all chronically online, but that doesn't mean we're truly connected to each other. We're growing apart, and we're not even noticing it.

Sending memes is not a replacement for conversations. You send tens of memes to your friends, and we barely even open all of them, let alone respond to each of them individually. Nobody has the time. We're mindlessly sending memes and tricking ourselves into believing we're maintaining friendships.

Friendships are about long phone calls and conversations over coffee in person. Friendships are about being there for each other when you need each other the most. Friendships are about knowing the details of each other's lives and being genuinely interested in knowing what the other person is up to. Memes aren't real conversations.

When was the last time you were vulnerable in front of a friend or a family member? When was the last time you asked someone how they were really doing?

9. LETTING ELDERS MAKE YOUR LIFE DECISIONS

My father studied engineering. My mother, law. My sister, medicine. And I'm an author. Science and math, commerce, science and biology and humanities—all in the same household. People are different, and when we embrace those differences instead of ensuring everybody does the same thing, we grow in life. This is what you need to understand:

- Your parents have your best interests at heart, but they may not be the best people to reach out to for career advice, especially if you're looking to make a career in a field they have no knowledge about. Please visit a career counsellor, and be very certain of what really gives you joy before choosing a career path. You don't need to have a career in a field you're not interested in just because someone in your family believes it's the best option for you. If it

doesn't align with your interests, it's not worth pursuing.
- Be very careful while choosing a life partner. Date for a few years and only then get married to someone. You don't just need to know someone before you marry them. You need to understand their heart. You deserve someone who stands with you even at your worst. Someone who respects your boundaries. Someone who values you at all times. Someone who loves you with their whole heart. Please choose your life partner by yourself. Don't pay heed to any persuasion. It's better to marry late than marry someone who isn't right for you.
- Just because your parents listened to your grandparents and allowed them to choose a partner for them doesn't mean you have to follow the same path. What worked for one generation may not work for the next, and that doesn't make you a bad child. It makes you a responsible adult who doesn't want to ruin his own life and that of another

person, only because he cares too much about societal expectations and norms.

- Your parents may have stayed in one city all their lives, and that may have worked out well for them, but you're not obligated to stay in the same city. You're not obligated to stop yourself from exploring opportunities just because it doesn't align with your parents.
- Your parents may have gotten married at twenty-four, and you may not even be thinking about it at twenty-six, and that's okay. They may have taken all their financial advice from their parents, but you want to hire a chartered accountant or a financial adviser, and that's okay. They may believe in astrology and you don't, and that's okay. They may not believe in therapy, and you do, and that's okay. The differences don't mean love doesn't exist. These differences just indicate a generational gap that can be dealt with kindness.

10. JEALOUSY AS A WAY OF BEING MOTIVATED

When you're jealous of someone, you subconsciously put them on a pedestal. You assume they have something unattainable. You assume they're better than you, and you can't bridge that gulf. You're not inspired, you're bitter. You don't wish to grow; you wish for them to fall. You become so obsessed with them that you forget that you're a unique individual with interests and dreams of your own, independent of that person. You forget that you're harming your peace and sanity by lending them space in your head. You constantly feel like you're not enough, even though everything they have achieved is achievable, but you don't need to run after it only because they have it. You don't need to run after anything you're not really passionate about, only because you're jealous someone else has it. You don't need to keep overthinking someone who's out there living their best life. They're growing because they're choosing what makes them happy, and you're choosing to compulsively keep a tab on everything they do instead of focusing on your goals, dreams and happiness. Stop hurting yourself like that.

10

STAGNANCY OR SELF-LOVE?

Healing doesn't come to you; you walk towards it, one step at a time.

During the lockdown, I gained a lot of weight. I wasn't exercising. I was scrolling all day long. I watched all the sitcoms available on the Internet.

When the lockdown was about to end, I looked at myself in the mirror and thought, *there's no way I can go out like this.* I hadn't shaved my beard in months. I hadn't gotten a haircut. I was a mess.

For the first three months after lockdown, my best friend kept convincing me to go to the gym with her. I would say things like:

- I don't have the energy for it (I was wasting all my energy on doomscrolling).
- I don't feel nice in the gym (I felt amazing at the gym. I just didn't want to go).
- I'd rather do brisk walking (at least that would change the topic).
- I'm not in the right state of mind for working out (I was overthinking all day about my weight).
- I love myself the way I am (I thought I could use self-love as an excuse to not work on my body).

When you're stuck in a routine—healthy or unhealthy—your brain keeps convincing you that staying comfortable is the most important thing in the world. And there's no comfort in change, only uncertainty. So even though I was smart enough to realize I was getting obese and needed to work on my body, my mind was becoming my worst enemy and trying to find ways to tell me that I didn't really need to work out.

This is what overthinking does to you. You know you need to change something, but the more you think about it, the more reasons your brain gives you to remain where you are—to remain stuck.

During the lockdown, I had inadvertently trained my body to refrain from any physical activity, and hence, my mind was convinced that this was the most comfortable way of being, and that's what I should chase.

This was my brush with feeling helpless. I refrained from looking at my body in the mirror because it broke my heart. This was just another way of avoiding reality and continuing to live a lifestyle that was slowly eating me up.

I realized I would do anything to avoid working out. I would watch hundreds of YouTube videos looking for motivation. I'd call my friends looking for motivation. And honestly, I knew I had to work on my body, but I simply couldn't figure out how to stop overthinking about how to make my body better and actually work on it.

Until one day, the lift in my apartment stopped working, and I had to climb three flights of stairs. My heartbeat didn't get back to normal for the next two hours. I thought I was having a heart attack. I lay in my bed without telling anybody what was happening inside me, because I didn't want them to say, 'I told you so.' I knew things were getting worse.

Later that day, I simply got up and went to the gym. I didn't think about anything. Best decision ever. I figured that overthinking leads to a cycle of analysis and paralysis: you keep overthinking, but don't take any action. You keep worrying about the problem at hand to the point where you don't actually end up doing anything to solve it. I was thinking so much about my increasing weight that I forgot that overthinking it wasn't reducing it. I was binge-eating because of anxiety. I was looking for an escape from the same thing I was trying to avoid—junk food. I was hoping to find a solution by overthinking my weight when the solution was right in front of me all along. I just had to get up and go to the gym.

Overthinking is not analysis. Overthinking is not productive. Overthinking breeds stagnancy. Sometimes, all you need to do is start working. Start working before your mind can convince you it's easier to stay where you are, the way you are. Start working before your overthinking takes over you. Not all your thoughts deserve your attention.

I was constantly fooling myself by saying that I loved myself, and that's why it didn't matter how my body looked. But in reality, I did not love myself. I didn't like how my body looked. I couldn't even look at myself in the mirror. It took me years to understand that self-love isn't about not changing yourself for the better. It's not about staying stuck in toxic loops and finding ways to romanticize the issues you don't want to confront. Self-love is about being kind to your body and mind, and knowing that your well-being is a priority, not an option. It's in respecting your body enough to keep it healthy. It's in respecting your mind enough to not overthink for hours. It's in breaking the pattern.

Self-love is in allowing yourself to change things about yourself that you can't seem to get comfortable with. The things that make you feel bad about yourself. The things that are affecting your confidence or health. Do everything that makes you feel more secure. If you're not okay with your skin, make skincare a priority. And while everyone can't afford expensive skincare, there are plenty of really effective home remedies available online. If you're not okay with your body, make working out an essential part of your routine. If you can't afford to go to the gym, choose running or playing a sport. If you're not okay with your hair, experiment with different hairstyles. If you think you aren't eloquent enough, join online courses or watch YouTube videos. Learn new words and practice the language. If you feel you're not good at any sport and really want to try, join an academy. Or go out and find clubs.

Just because you are uncomfortable about a specific attribute about yourself doesn't mean you don't love yourself. You're allowed to become the person you have always dreamt of becoming and take the necessary steps for the same without feeling guilty about it. Only a person who loves themselves cares enough to work on themselves.

Another reason why the entire idea of forcing yourself to be happy and content the way you are doesn't work in the real world is because humans aren't islands. We do not exist in isolation. There are rules—some really unfortunate and unfair—but we can't ignore their existence, and we can't run away from them.

Based on where you live, there are beauty standards. Models, actors and influencers reinforce them. Unrealistic body standards are normalized. Pretty privilege is real. The key is not to give in to all the unrealistic beauty standards—it is to ensure you're being the best version of yourself and that you feel secure every day.

People keep talking about inner beauty, but the sad truth is that all dating apps require your photographs. Being someone's 'crush' requires a certain physical appearance. And as much as we don't want these things to get to us, they do impact us in more ways than one. Conventionally attractive people receive more attention and opportunities than others. They do get treated better. It's easier for them to make friends and get into relationships. It's unfair, but it's true.

Every time you see posts by influencers, you wonder how to look like them. You start being critical of your natural features. You compare yourself with everybody on the Internet. The protagonists of movies don't have acne or stretch marks. They speak perfectly, and their hair flows beautifully. There's very little representation in the media of how most people look in real life.

The truth is, this might change, but it's going to take a long time.

Here's what you need to understand:

- Chasing beauty standards is useless because they keep changing. People who are considered pretty in one culture may not be considered attractive in another.
- You need to work on your body to ensure you stay fit and healthy. You don't necessarily need to have six-pack abs or a chiselled jawline to be healthy. Respecting your body does not mean blindly following beauty standards.
- You must work to become the best version of yourself. The understanding that you respect yourself enough to embark on a journey of self-improvement (unlike most people out there) will ensure you feel confident in every room.
- The world will keep finding ways to make you feel bad about yourself. As long as your physical and mental health are well-

tended to, you don't need to pay heed to the opinions around you.
- Just because you want to change something about your appearance doesn't mean you don't love yourself. Only a self-loving person wants to feel better about themselves while being kind to all versions of themselves.
- Capitalism thrives on making people insecure about themselves. Please know that your worth isn't determined by how similar you look to an influencer, actor or model. How you feel within matters more than how capitalists are determined to make you feel. If you're working on yourself and know that you're physically fit and taking care of yourself, nothing else really matters.

In conclusion, it's hard not to tie your self-worth to your appearance in a world obsessed with beauty. It's harder not to lose yourself in the process. But every time you choose progress over perfection, knowing perfection is a I, you sow the seeds of confidence within yourself.

11

SELF-LOVE IS (NOT) ENOUGH

Everybody on the Internet is obsessed with the idea of being alone. There are hundreds of videos on the topic, and many books about the same. But I believe there's a major misunderstanding about the entire concept of self-love that people are unwilling to address.

In 2022, my feed was swamped by 'solo date' ideas. I was single and didn't have many friends. I wondered if that would be a fun way for me to explore new places by myself. But here's the thing—I went to a café alone, and it felt terrible. I did not enjoy it. I felt embarrassed, awkward and uncomfortable. The waiters weren't nice either. Three of them asked if I was expecting company, and when I said no, I saw a look on their face I really didn't like. It was a mix of confusion and sympathy. I wanted to enjoy my meal, take pictures and post them online, but I felt so terrible that I quickly ate the fries I had ordered and left.

I went back home and read a post online about how solo dates can be uncomfortable at first, but eventually, you start loving them. I went on multiple solo dates in the next three months. Each time, I felt more terrible than before. I simply couldn't romanticize being by myself and eating alone. Or exploring a museum by myself. Or going to a concert alone.

I kept overthinking, wondering why I wasn't able to enjoy solo dates. I asked myself, *is it because I don't love myself?* But the answer was right there. No. It wasn't the absence of self-love but a genuine yearning for connections, love and friendships. I loved myself, and that's why I stopped going out on solo dates once I realized they were not the right fit for me. I loved myself, and that's why I stopped making myself miserable by forcing myself to enjoy and romanticize something I truly didn't. The Internet has normalized generalizing notions that may or may not be valid for everyone.

I love to have conversations. I love meeting new people. When I'm at a concert, I want to wrap my arms around someone and scream the lyrics together. When I'm at a café, I want to sit with a friend and discuss crushes, TV shows or that one person from high school we both didn't like. My inability to enjoy a solo date didn't imply an absence of self-love. My love for myself is not defined by my ability to romanticize whatever the Internet wants me to romanticize.

Ever since I was four, my grandfather had made it a point to always talk to me in English. He wanted me to be fluent in it. Back then, I lived in a small town where the kids weren't kind to me for not being like them. They made me feel terrible for being myself. They loved to play cricket. I didn't. They judged me for speaking English. They labelled me as arrogant for speaking in a language I was comfortable in, in an English-medium school. Hysterical, now that I think about it. They judged me for watching *Hannah Montana* because they thought it was too 'girly'. I can't believe I was bullied for watching a television show. My parents didn't allow me to hang out with people after school because they wanted me to focus on academics, and hence, after school, I had no chance of making any friends or strengthening existing friendships. Honestly, I didn't like those kids anyway.

Growing up, I have realized my most miserable years were marked by the absence of good friends. For a major part of my childhood and throughout my teenage years, I remained hyper-dependent on my parents emotionally because I had no friends. And that made me put them on a pedestal. Every time my mom would scold me, I would overthink and cry incessantly. I'd feel like she'd leave me. I'd feel unwanted.

After taking therapy, I saw how I was putting way too much pressure on my mother for being perfect because I simply didn't have anybody else in my life who would make me feel loved. People are allowed to mess up, make mistakes, get angry and feel overwhelmed. But when you put the burden of ensuring you feel happy on one person alone—it suffocates them. Given the hyper-dependence, you panic and overthink even the minutest change in their behaviour.

And so, in the eleventh standard, when I switched schools, and I realized I wasn't in a conservative set-up any more, I found the right set of friends, and my entire life changed. When I found good friends, I could now go to them for advice. I could call them and speak my heart out. I could go out with them when I wouldn't feel okay. I realized I needed people. I now believe everyone needs people.

Feeling lonely or being socially disconnected can have catastrophic consequences on your health. It can even increase your chances of dying early. Researchers studied over 3.4 million people across seventy studies for about seven years, and this is what they found:

- People who felt lonely were 26 per cent more likely to die early.
- Socially isolated people were 29 per cent more likely to die early.
- People who lived alone had a 32 per cent chance of early death.

The entire concept of isolation and finding joy in isolation doesn't sit right with me. I can sit by myself and complete my work. I can stay at home, order a nice meal for myself and relish it. But I'd be lying if I said I feel like I don't need anybody. Or that I'm enough for myself. I need people, and there's no shame in acknowledging the same. The feeling of not having a bunch of genuine friends in my life is extremely unsettling for me, and while I'm very selective about who I choose to be friends with, I always ensure I'm connecting with people who I feel truly deserve my time, energy and attention. If you're someone who can relate to this, please know that there's absolutely no need to coerce yourself into enjoying solo dates if you don't want to. There's no reason to isolate yourself trying to enjoy 'solitude' when you know that you miss having a best friend or a partner.

Self-love is not enough. You need people who care about you to stay focused and sane. Loneliness and isolation are terrible for your mental health in the long run. People say when you're alone, you focus on growth and get better than before. But in all honesty, I have realized that when you're loved the right way, that's when you truly focus on your growth and get closer and closer to becoming your best self. And that love doesn't have to essentially be romantic. There are oceans of love in friendships, too.

When you know that there's someone out there who'll love you just as much, even if you mess up or fail, that there's someone who'll be there for you each step of the way, you achieve a whole other level of confidence. When someone else believes in you, your belief in your abilities increases, too. Self-love is about believing in yourself and your abilities, but trust me, having someone who loves you enough to support you in all the right ways, trusts your talent and reminds you of your worth, makes you love yourself way more than you already do.

Also, I believe the idea of 'I'm enough for myself' somehow ends up making you weak instead of stronger. Because you then hesitate to ask for help. You feel the burden of figuring everything out on your own. You refuse to believe that you're only human, and there are a lot of situations that you cannot handle alone. And when you think this way, you feel lonelier than ever in times of crisis because you have got it in your head that strong/self-loving people don't need other people, which is not true.

Self-love is:

- Believing in yourself with your whole heart, but not being afraid of acknowledging

that sometimes it does feel better to hear it from someone else, and not feel guilty about it.
- Keeping your heart open to genuine friendships and relationships that add to your happiness instead of assuming the responsibility of always ensuring you're happy and not letting anybody else be the reason for your happiness sometimes.
- Loving the ones who love you with all honesty. There are people out there whose lives wouldn't be the same without you. There are people out there who love you so much that they want to support you and help you grow, and you must always show gratitude towards them.
- Accepting that not everyone can do everything. When a book is written, one person writes the content, another person proofreads it, a company publishes it and another distributes it. And you know what happens when one person tries to do it all? The book doesn't achieve its full potential.

- Do not be afraid of accepting and asking for help.
- Knowing that sometimes all you need is to be held with love, and there's nothing wrong with wanting that.

Self-love is not always a table for one and a single movie ticket. Sometimes it's in accepting that you're a table-for-two person, and you love to share your popcorn during movies.

You're worthy of not just your own love but also the love that others have to offer you. You deserve shared laughter and happiness. You deserve to fall into the arms of someone willing to hold you gently. You don't have to do it all alone. You're not a machine. You have feelings that are sometimes best dealt with when shared with someone else, and that's okay. Keep your heart open to love, always.

12

CAN'T CROSS MY BOUNDARIES

Here are signs that you respect yourself—mind, body and soul:

1. You create a routine for yourself. When I say routine, I do not mean every hour of your day is devoted to a specific activity. A routine means having a set of activities every day that you simply never skip. Skincare, going for a walk or working out, for instance. People who respect themselves have a schedule they follow, come what may.

2. You do not skip taking a shower. Not allowing yourself to lie in bed overthinking and going to take a shower to get out of the loop of anxious thoughts is extremely important.
3. You do not mind saying goodbye to the people who don't treat you the right way.
4. You create boundaries that nobody is allowed to cross, no matter how close they are to you. You only allow people to get closer to you when they fully understand and respect your boundaries and non-negotiables.
5. Whenever you step out of your house, you're well-dressed. A person who respects themselves won't ever go out shabbily dressed. First impressions are generally based on appearances and outfits, and you must look like someone who cares about looking presentable by dressing sharply. Nails trimmed, hair styled properly, shoes polished, outfit ironed and accessories on point.

6. You call people out when they try to make you feel bad about yourself by cracking 'jokes' at your expense or passing comments for 'fun'. You don't entertain people who don't know how to be funny without being mean to the people around them. There's no room for scapegoat humour in your life.
7. You respect your body enough not to consume drugs. You don't believe substance abuse is essential for having a 'good time'.
8. You don't feed your mind with negative self-talk, and always speak highly of yourself. You believe in yourself even when the world refuses to believe in you. You are your loudest cheerleader at all times.
9. You stop making efforts for people when it's not reciprocated or taken for granted. You know that you bring a lot to the table and act accordingly. Anybody who doesn't cherish you doesn't get access to you.
10. You don't put the kind of food in your body that makes you anxious/is harmful to your health. I have seen people with high sugar

levels refusing to give up sweets. I have seen people who get anxious every time they have coffee fill their bodies with caffeine. Don't be such a person. Your body is on your team. Value it. I'm not advising you to quit fast food altogether. I'm just asking you to limit the consumption of what harms you.

11. You refuse to be disrespected at work. You believe that you're a magnet for opportunities, and someone's inability to see your worth doesn't define your value. You call out toxic managers, don't engage in office politics for the sake of your own peace, give your best at work and don't mind walking away when your efforts aren't valued.

12. You don't give second chances easily. When you remove someone from your life, it takes a lot more than a simple apology for you to consider taking someone back in. You don't treat yourself like a hotel room where people can check-in and check-out at any time. You get to decide who stays in your life and for

how long. People have to earn a space in your heart.
13. You don't give up on hobbies that you can't/don't want to monetize. If you like crocheting, you take out time to do it. If you like swimming, you go for a swim now and then. You do not give up on your hobbies because you don't give in to the capitalistic idea of turning everything into a source of income and discarding whatever isn't.
14. Stephen R. Covey, in his book *The 7 Habits of Highly Effective People*, talks about two mindsets—the abundance mindset and the scarcity mindset. The people who love and respect themselves have an abundance mindset i.e. they believe there's an abundance of love, opportunities and resources in the world, so someone else's victory doesn't equate to their defeat. There's no room for jealousy because everything exists in abundance. On the other hand, a person with a scarcity mindset believes that

success is a finite resource. They're pissed off by other people's achievements because they do not believe there's enough money, opportunities or love in the world for everyone. An abundance mindset will save you from the toxic hate and envy people carry within themselves. It'll save you from believing someone else's happiness can take away yours.

15. You're not rigid. You're open to new perspectives. You don't reject other people's opinions just because they are different from yours. You're a good listener, not a know-it-all. You genuinely want to keep growing and learning new things.
16. You keep the space around you clean. You don't sit on an unmade bed. You don't leave the utensils in the kitchen unwashed for days. You arrange your wardrobe every once in a while. You don't delay discarding leftover food. You change your bedsheets when they get dirty without delaying it. Your desk is always organized.

17. You're always hydrated. You carry a water bottle with you wherever you go.
18. You don't romanticize having a messed-up sleep schedule. You sleep on time because you respect your body to understand that it deserves to rest.
19. You don't indulge in doomscrolling all day long. You try to spend your time doing more meaningful things—spending time with your loved ones, reading a book, going out for a walk or watching a movie.
20. You're never ungrateful. Even on your worst days, you don't forget that life can't always suck. You remember everything you have achieved and never think less of yourself.
21. You firmly believe you have it in you to achieve everything you want to achieve and don't mind putting in the work to make it happen.
22. You don't go back to your ex-partners hoping to make things better. You respect yourself enough to know that you don't need anybody who doesn't want you.

23. You don't create versions of people in your head and romanticize them for the potential you see in them. Instead, you judge people by their actions. You see them for who they are. You know that words mean nothing unless they're supported by actions.
24. You don't stop believing in love just because an idiot couldn't love you the right way.
25. You don't take rejection to heart because you believe there are ample opportunities in the world, and everything you deserve will find you eventually.
26. You don't stay silent in rooms just because someone else is too loud. You don't shrink yourself. You voice your opinions with confidence because you know they matter. You know you matter.
27. Someone's disbelief in you doesn't dictate your life choices. Whatever you believe in with conviction is done by you, even if the only person who thinks it's a good idea is you.
28. You don't force yourself to be productive at the expense of your mental health. Your

career doesn't matter more than your sanity. You don't feel guilty about taking breaks because you never let capitalism convince you that it's okay to torture yourself to be more productive. You're not a machine.

29. You don't force someone to like you. You can admire someone and try to talk to them, but if they do not seem to care, you don't keep trying to impress them. You don't chase people, knowing well enough that there are over 8 billion individuals in this world, and one person's decision to not like you or befriend you really doesn't matter.

30. You don't get angry easily. You choose distance instead of unnecessary toxicity. You don't waste your energy on the people who don't have the emotional intelligence to comprehend things.

31. You don't try to keep fixing someone unwilling to change for the better. That one friend who keeps coming to you for advice but never takes it. That one colleague who keeps criticizing his girlfriend but doesn't

ever want to walk away. You don't need to waste your time guiding people who simply want to rant without doing anything about their problems.
32. You don't tolerate people who keep playing victim after hurting you. There's no room for gaslighting in your life. You'd rather live without them than put up with their manipulation. Someone who cannot take accountability for their actions and apologize even when they're in the wrong doesn't deserve to stay in your life.
33. You never take your wins for granted. You never tell people that it was luck when it was sheer hard work. You never downplay your achievements because the people sitting in front of you haven't achieved as much. If you feel the need to downplay your achievements, you know that you're sitting at the wrong table.
34. You don't remain friends with people you're scared of sharing good news with. If you can't call them the moment you have

good news, your heart knows they're secretly jealous of you and don't want you to grow in life. If you don't believe they'll be happy to see you grow, don't think twice before distancing yourself from them.

35. You don't mind expressing your needs in any relationship. If birthdays are a big deal for you, you make sure they know it. If you're someone who loves to travel, make sure they know it.

36. You don't stop yourself from crying because you know vulnerability makes you human, and feeling sad is completely normal. You don't live with the pain. You let it all out.

37. You don't make plans with people who never initiate plans with you. You're never the only one trying.

38. You're not scared of being disliked for having boundaries. You'd rather be disliked from a distance than disrespected in person.

39. You don't let your trauma shape your entire life. You seek help whenever required. You reassure yourself that you deserve the best

things in life. You're patient with your journey.

40. You don't overthink for hours about things that aren't in your control. You trust your journey and know that great things are in store for you.

13

OVERTHINKING? OVER IT.

'**W**ould you call yourself an overthinker?' In a poll I conducted online, out of the 5408 participants, 5100 (94.3 per cent) responded with a 'yes' and only 308 (5.7 per cent) responded 'no'. This data made me feel less alone. I realized overthinking is a shared experience, but the good news is that it's not impossible to overcome.

Over the years, I have tried a lot of things to overcome my habit of overthinking, but the following are the techniques that helped me the most. I hope they help you too!

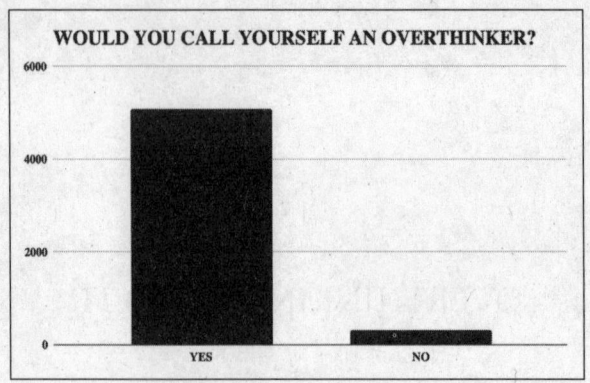

1. THE S.S.E. RULE: STUPID-SENSIBLE-EXPLANATION

- **How it works:**
  - When you catch yourself overthinking, grab a pen and paper and make three columns:
    - Column 1: Stupid
    - Column 2: Sensible
    - Column 3: Explanation
  - Write down the thought that's making you anxious in the sensible section.
  - Give yourself sixty seconds to come up with a logical explanation to justify the thought using facts, not feelings.

- If even after sixty seconds you fail to come up with a logical explanation, the thought in your head deserves to be moved into the stupid category. Strike it off from the sensible section, and place it where it belongs.
- This will help you pause and think logically instead of letting your anxious thoughts convince you that the worst-case scenario is the only scenario likely to happen.

2. THE 99 PER CENT RULE

- **How it works:**
  - Assume that 99 per cent of your fears might actually come true.
  - The 99 per cent rule focuses on the remaining 1 per cent—the possibility of it all just being in your head.
  - Focus on the 1 per cent for ninety-nine seconds. Let it breathe. Don't dismiss it as unrealistic. In those ninety-nine seconds, there's only a 1 per cent possibility of things not falling apart.

- This way, you do not dismiss the fear completely, but stop it from feeling like the reality by leaving a 1 per cent window—and sometimes that's enough to get you out of a toxic loop.
- For example, Kartik is overthinking a presentation. He's convinced he's going to mess up. But for ninety-nine seconds, he gives a chance to the possibility of not messing up, and in fact, acing the presentation. He's no longer acting like the worst-case scenario is the only outcome possible, and that's no less than a victory in itself.

3. THE S.I.P. RULE: SIP WATER–INITIATE A CONVERSATION–PHYSICALLY MOVE

- **How it works:**
  - **Sip water:** When you realize you're overthinking again, take a sip of water. Don't rush. Focus on the water for a moment.

- **Initiate a conversation:** Once you're done, immediately call someone/talk to someone at home. The conversation doesn't have to be about what you're overthinking. This will help you change your focus.
- **Physically move:** Once you're done conversing, go for a walk, stretch your arms and legs or clean your room. Even light movement can shift your focus and calm yourself. It's like saying to your brain, 'We're okay now.'

4. THE C.A.L.L. RULE: CONFRONT- ARTICULATE-LISTEN- LEAVE

- **How it works:**
  - Get on a fake phone call with yourself and put how you're feeling into words, unapologetically.
  - **Confront:** Face the feeling. Say it out loud without sugarcoating it or lying to yourself. For instance, I'm feeling like I'll lose my job. I'm feeling like I'm not

good enough for anyone. I feel like my girlfriend is going to leave me.
- **Articulate:** Explain to yourself why you feel the way you do—calmly and in as much detail as possible. Maybe you fought with a friend or had a bad day at work. Explain your situation in detail.
- **Listen:** Switch sides—become the best friend on the other side of the call. Give yourself advice like you'd do to someone you love. Don't judge. React with empathy. Focus on finding a solution.
- **Leave:** Once you have said everything you need to, step away from the space. Leave the room. Engage in a totally different activity like watching a movie, going out for a walk or playing your favourite music.
- When you consciously try to understand your overthinking instead of assuming it's the gospel truth, you separate yourself from the chaos in your head.

Overthinking can't be overcome overnight, since it's a habit you have developed and lived with for years. But every small step counts. Every time you use one of these techniques, you send a message to your brain that not all anxious thoughts are rooted in reality. Not all the stories in your head are true. Whenever you find yourself in chaos, I hope you use these techniques to feel lighter. You have got this!

14

EVERYTHING'S FINE, BUT IS IT?

Imagine this: Rhea decides to write a book. She takes a few writing courses, reads a lot of books and now feels ready to finally start working on her own. But while she's yet to start working on the first draft, she's already worrying about whether or not her dream publishing house will be willing to publish it. She keeps overthinking what would happen if they reject her work. She thinks about all those emails that she'd send that might never get a reply. She feels too demotivated to even start writing the book. She keeps delaying writing the book as a coping mechanism to avoid the rejection she was expecting.

Rhea's situation can be seen as an example of self-handicapping, a strategy where people try to create problems for themselves so that if/when they fail, they can blame it on the problems instead of questioning their merit/worth. This theory was introduced by Edward E. Jones and Steven Berglas in 1978. Rhea was scared of rejection, and so, she kept creating scenarios in her head and eventually quit. By not writing at all, she saved herself from a rejection that wasn't even guaranteed.

If Rhea had focused on writing the first draft, paying full attention to the quality of her work instead of worrying about what would happen to her work in the future, even if she hadn't gotten a publishing deal, she'd have her book ready with her. Overthinking it and giving in to the fear of rejection left her with neither a publishing deal nor a book to get a deal on.

Other examples of self-handicapping include saying 'yes' to plans right before exams and later on blaming them for your bad grades, calling a friend and gossiping with them for hours right before the day of an important interview and then blaming the phone call in case you don't get the job, deliberately skipping going on a date with someone you really like because you're scared it won't go well etc. You avoid focusing on what truly matters because you're scared of failure, and you actively look for reasons you'll use in the future to justify the failure in case it happens.

Mindfulness expert Jon Kabat-Zinn talks about the 'doing mode' and 'being mode'. Doing mode is when you're focusing on a task at hand, trying to get it done. It's like when you're solving a sudoku, finishing a report or answering emails.

Being mode, on the other hand, is when you're relishing a cup of coffee, listening to the sound of the birds, watching the scenery or taking a walk. Being mode is about being in the moment without trying to be productive.

You need to understand that you can't always remain in the doing mode. You need to exist without wanting to be productive, worrying about the future or dwelling in the past. When was the last time you watched the sunset? When was the last time you truly relished a meal without thinking about some other due task/chore? When was the last time you went on a vacation and truly left work behind? When was the last time you enjoyed your morning coffee without replying to emails simultaneously?

Overthinking the future is the easiest way to make yourself upset about things that haven't even happened yet and might never happen. Why are you stealing your own joy by creating scenarios in your head that are not based on reason or facts?

Overthinking the past doesn't make sense because time machines aren't real, and there's no way you can change what's already happened. What you could've done differently is irrelevant since the past is done and dusted. You have been through so much in the past, but you're still here—you need to move ahead instead of succumbing to the irrational thoughts that keep you tied to your past. This is what you need to remember:

When you have a task in hand, focus on what's really in your control. In Rhea's case, the things she could control were the title, themes, length and quality of her work, and the emails she'd eventually write to publishing houses. But she was too busy focusing on rejection. Instead of believing in her skills and talents and completing the first draft, she was drowning in anxiety over scenarios that existed only in her head. Focusing on what's in your control eliminates room for the inconsequential. When you allow your thoughts to run wild instead of being present in the moment, you end up ruining something that could've been amazing.

Don't miss out on living your life because you're always worried about what might go wrong or what has already gone wrong. So many of us live too little and worry too much. Don't lose yourself to the irrational thoughts that are stopping you from living your best life.

15

CHRONICALLY (ANXIOUS) ONLINE

You wake up, and the first thing you do is look for your phone. Probably right after putting on the glasses you probably wouldn't need if it weren't for your phone. Once you have the phone in your hands, your glasses on and your eyes barely open, you begin looking at notifications, knowing very well there's nothing so important that it can't wait until you have gotten out of bed and freshened up. Most people use their phones even in the restroom. People start scrolling right when the day begins and keep doing it whenever they find an opportunity during the day. The other day, I booked a cab, and the driver was scrolling while driving. This is alarming and extremely dangerous.

The videos are getting shorter than ever. And even those videos are hard to watch because we lack focus. Algorithms intend to keep giving your brain dopamine, the feel-good neurotransmitter. The more you scroll, the more you feel like continuing. Algorithms show you content similar to what you engage with the most, and hence, you get access to thousands of videos every day that are unimportant but keep you hooked for hours.

Here are the problems with scrolling:

1. You don't need that much information. We're getting bombarded with irrelevant, inconsequential, uninspiring information every single minute, and we've so much of it in our heads that we can't seem to really focus on anything in real life. Your mind doesn't get enough rest, and your brain is working overtime.

2. The Internet pushes a lot of content that adds no value to your life. Self-deprecating humour, problematic opinions and insensitive comments. You fill your head with so much negativity that positive affirmations don't make sense to you.
3. Algorithms are designed to trigger dopamine as you scroll. While you're scrolling, you feel this urge to keep going until you get the dopamine they have made you accustomed to receiving. When you're offline, you crave the same dopamine.
4. Algorithms push beauty standards and 'thirst traps' that make you question your self-worth. You see perfectly curated lives and wonder why yours doesn't look the same. You start questioning your life choices because you're stuck in a comparison loop where your anxiety convinces you that everyone on the Internet is doing better than you.
5. You gradually lose the patience and focus it takes to enjoy a really good book or a movie

without scrolling simultaneously, skipping half of it or avoiding it altogether. You look for fifteen seconds of entertainment everywhere instead of savouring art patiently.
6. You don't retain information easily any more. If I ask you to tell me the last ten videos you watched on the Internet, chances are, most of you won't even remember the last two or three videos. We're all doomscrolling without even realizing its consequences.
7. When you're scrolling, you're separating yourself from the present, which can be a memory you would've cherished for a long time if it weren't for the fact that you were too busy being online. For instance, a family dinner where everyone's laughing but you're replying to messages. A movie date with your partner where you check your phone every five minutes.
8. Social media shows you content without you having much control over what you see and what you don't. Sometimes, the algorithm

ends up showing you content that triggers your anxiety or reminds you of a traumatic experience. Posts about friendship when you're fighting with your best friend can make you feel worse about your situation. A post about someone's grandparents who passed away recently can trigger your fear of losing your grandparents.

9. There's way too much unregulated and dangerous advice on the Internet. Random people predicting your future. Misinformation in the name of news. Hate-inducing lies. All of it is extremely problematic and misleading.
10. You spend so much time and energy focusing on the irrelevant that there's barely any time or energy left for the things and people that truly matter to you.

The truth is, the Internet is lying to you. Algorithms are tricking you into believing you need all that information when you really don't. Please set a limit on your social media consumption. Please don't fill your head with information that doesn't add any value to your life. Please save yourself from the web to really be able to live your life to the fullest.

16

SLEEP ON TIME (CAN'T BELIEVE MOM WAS RIGHT!)

As kids, we went to school every day. We'd wake up at 6 a.m., brush our teeth, get ready and leave. Now, if someone asks us to get up that early, we find it preposterous. Why? Because we're not used to that schedule any more. However, we followed it for years, and it's not like we're incapable of getting up at 6 a.m. again; it's just that now we have the choice to not do it.

Having a choice isn't always a good thing. Let me explain. We don't work out because nobody's going to punish us for not working out. We don't realize that the punishment for not working out is deteriorating health. We don't focus on the long-term consequences of things because in the present, there seem to be no consequences for the same. We skip meals because nobody's going to scold us if we do. We rot in bed all weekend after deciding to café hop or explore new places because there are no consequences for the same. Our moms keep asking us to have a routine, but we never listen.

The key to having a routine is being accountable. For instance, every time I skip my skincare, I send Rs 500 to my sister, who I know will never return it. So, every time I'm being lazy, there's a definite price I have to pay for it. Also, the price should really matter to you. It shouldn't be inconsequential. For instance, if I had to just pay her Rs 50 instead of Rs 500, on days when I'd feel too lazy to do my skincare, I'd simply send her that money, thereby defeating the entire purpose. Sometimes knowing something is good for you doesn't motivate you enough to actually do it. Sometimes you need to lose something or get scolded to stick to something you really want to do.

Every time I'm working on a deadline, my best friend motivates me to stick to the deadline by giving me something when I complete it. For instance, if I complete writing a book by x date, she'd take a few days off work and plan a long vacation with me the same month. If I don't, the vacation remains cancelled for the next three months. No amount of convincing from my end makes her reconsider. I don't get offended because I know it's for my own good.

B.F. Skinner, an American psychologist and behaviourist, developed the ideas of positive and negative reinforcement. The word 'reinforcement' means making something stronger. It basically means that when you reward or punish a behaviour, it becomes stronger or weaker.

Positive reinforcement is when your boss makes you the employee of the month for your hard work. You feel motivated to work just as well or even better, the next month. It's when your teacher gives a star with your marks when you score well to motivate you to do it again.

Negative reinforcement is when you know that if you do something that's not supposed to be done, you'll be scolded/punished. For example, a child cleans his room before his parents come back from work because he knows his mom will scold him if he doesn't. A student is not allowed to sit in an exam if they haven't fulfilled the attendance requirements for the semester.

Both are important and effective, and depending on what works best for you, you should integrate them into your life to ensure you stick to a routine. As children, during summer vacations, we'd make schedules on paper where we'd allocate time for going to the park, learning a new skill and completing homework. None of us would stick to the schedule. As adults, we make plans to practice an instrument, save money for going on a vacation or complete projects on time, but to no avail. Sometimes the importance of something is enhanced when there's a price to pay or an award to receive.

Having a routine is extremely important because, as the proverb goes, 'An empty mind is the devil's workshop.' When you don't have a schedule, you unknowingly end up scrolling or overthinking for hours. You keep creating scenarios in your head in your spare time because you have not allocated that time to anything. But when you know that it's 5 p.m. and you have to hit the gym or there will be a price to pay, you get up and go there, breaking the loop of overthinking. When you exercise, your body releases several hormones and neurochemicals like endorphins (the feel-good hormones) and serotonin (the mood stabilizer), and they reduce overthinking and anxiety. When you spend your time engaged in an activity that actively helps you get fitter while also positively impacting your mental health, you slowly distance yourself from the habit of overthinking.

According to psychologist Rachel Goldman, 'When people don't have a routine or structure to their day, it can cause increased stress and anxiety, as well as overwhelming feelings, lack of concentration, and focus.' When your time is allocated to mandatory activities, your focus remains on the next task at hand instead of listing what has happened in the past or might happen in the distant future. The more you stick to your schedule, the better you feel because your brain gets a feeling of accomplishment every time you don't give in to your overthinking/anxiety and stick to what you really want to do.

The key to sticking to a schedule, other than reinforcement, is not having a schedule that you hate. If you don't like working out, start with three to four days a week. Don't pressurize yourself to lift heavy weights initially. Make it as enjoyable and light as possible. Showing up is important. It's a prerequisite for progress. If you're hard on yourself by putting the pressure of achieving results right from the get-go, there's a huge possibility that you'll quit altogether.

If you decide to learn a new instrument, sitting down and trying to learn it is as applaudable as actually learning it. It's important not to diminish the progress in your head because that'd demotivate you and persuade you to quit.

You don't need to wake up at 5 a.m. to change your life. You don't need to torture yourself unnecessarily. You don't need to plan every minute of your day. List a few activities for each day that you're not supposed to skip, strike them off once done and you're good to go.

Building a routine takes time. The trick is to make it fun. And even if you fail to follow your schedule initially, it doesn't mean you don't have it in you to stick to one. Never forget, you got up for school at 6 a.m. for years. You prepared for exams for years. You got to work on time because you had to. You have it in you to be disciplined again, to do the things that aren't mandatory by making them mandatory, all for your own good.

17

SABOTAGE: MADE AT HOME, WITH LOVE

Self-sabotage is when you consciously or unconsciously end up doing things that hinder your growth and affect your mental health negatively. Sometimes you don't even realize you're engaging in self-sabotaging behaviour and keep swimming in the sea of negativity. These are the signs that you're being your own worst enemy:

- **THE PATTERN:** You hoard stuff given by your exes and keep revisiting it.

THE PATH FORWARD: When someone hurts you and you decide to let go of them, please let go of them, either fully or not at all. You don't need to be stuck in a place where you miss them, but you also know they have hurt you a lot. Don't hurt yourself by holding on to the past. Delete photographs. Discard gifts. Block them from everywhere—and stick to it.

- **THE PATTERN:** You keep trying to please people.
  THE PATH FORWARD: I had a friend who hated the idea of clubbing, but she'd still never say no to us. She'd be miserable at the club, but she'd say that she wanted to come with us. She was a people-pleaser who simply couldn't say no, even if it was at the expense of her peace. Don't be that person. Prioritize yourself, and please know that if your friends can't respect your boundaries or understand what makes you uncomfortable and if saying 'no' to a plan

can strain your relationship with them, it's not friendship at all. Say 'no' more often, unapologetically. The right people will respect you for it.

- **THE PATTERN:** You overcomplicate everything by letting your emotions take over you, without caring about the practical aspects of the situation and analysing it from a point of logic and reason.
THE PATH FORWARD: Feelings aren't facts. Giving in to your emotions isn't the best approach. For instance, if someone doesn't invite you to a party, you wonder what you have done wrong, label yourself boring and overthink it for hours. All this instead of simply understanding that the only way to find out is to approach the friend who didn't invite you. Talk to them as soon as possible. Ask yourself, what can I do to find my answers? What can I do to check if my thoughts are facts? Do exactly that.

- **THE PATTERN:** You ignore micro-toxicity. You allow people to give you the silent treatment. You act okay even when you're offended. When someone interrupts you in the middle of a conversation, you don't call them out.
  THE PATH FORWARD: It's better to create a scene than be disrespected all the time. Just because someone's not doing anything really terrible doesn't mean you have to wait for them to do it. You're allowed to call out unacceptable behaviour, no matter the intensity of it.

- **THE PATTERN:** You put yourself at the bottom of your priority list.
  THE PATH FORWARD: You are just as important as the people you love. It's okay to stop showing up for people for a while when your heart is feeling heavy. Spend money on yourself. Order your favourite food. Put your own needs first. Normalize taking care of yourself like you do for the ones you love.

- **THE PATTERN:** You forgive people even when the apology isn't genuine enough because you'd rather forgive than confront. You don't want to be the villain in any circumstance, even if it means speaking up for yourself.

  THE PATH FORWARD: You cannot make everyone like you. Sometimes people hurt you, and they don't even feel guilty about it. They don't regret their actions. They come back only to hurt you all over again. If the apology isn't genuine, you don't owe them forgiveness. And if they have hurt you to the point where you can't trust them again, don't feel obligated to keep them in your life just because they have apologized to you.

- **THE PATTERN:** You keep a tab on your exes/ex-best friends – who they're following or unfollowing, the places they're visiting or the companies they're working at. You re-read old messages and listen to old voice notes.

THE PATH FORWARD: The people you're still hung up on are not in your life any more for a reason. You don't deserve to hurt yourself over someone who couldn't value you when they had you in their life. People who really love you won't keep hurting you. Every time you stalk them online, you disrespect yourself. They couldn't treat you the right way, and that should be enough closure for you.

- **THE PATTERN:** You feel like you have to shrink yourself for people to find you lovable. You think that if you present your opinions or do not seek their validation, they'd not want to be friends with you.

  THE PATH FORWARD: Nobody's validation is important enough for you to stop staying true to yourself. You're not supposed to fit into a box; they want you to stay in only because that's ideal for them. If someone wants you to agree to everything they say, they think they're better than you, and you must never be friends with people who are too full of themselves to accept a difference of opinion.

- **THE PATTERN:** You lie to yourself. You promise yourself to follow a schedule or break a pattern, but don't actually end up doing it. You choose comfort, even if it comes at the expense of your physical or mental health.
THE PATH FORWARD: Love yourself enough to prioritize what truly matters for your well-being. A stitch in time saves nine. Your future self will thank you for caring about your wellness.

- **THE PATTERN:** You think you're unlucky or doomed. You blame your stars for everything that goes wrong in your life.
THE PATH FORWARD: Please know that you're the child of the universe, and the universe is always looking after you. Setbacks don't define your destiny. Make

a list of everyone in life you're grateful for and everything you have achieved since childhood. You're not unlucky. You just haven't realized the power of your potential yet.

- **THE PATTERN:** You never celebrate your achievements and stop yourself from dreaming big because you diminish your worth in your head.
  THE PATH FORWARD: Even the smallest of achievements are worth celebrating. Every time you make a mistake, you fixate on it for weeks, but when you achieve something, you don't feel like celebrating it. You owe it to yourself to take pride in what you have worked hard for.

- **THE PATTERN:** You're your biggest critic to the point where everything you do, you do it with the fear of failure crippling in.
  THE PATH FORWARD: There are way too many people in this world who'll try

to pull you down and make you feel bad about yourself. The world can be harsh, but you need to be kind to yourself. Be a cheerleader, not a critic.

- **THE PATTERN:** You listen to the opinions of others and shape your life according to their expectations.
THE PATH FORWARD: People are entitled to their opinions, but you don't have to pay heed to them. Most people don't know what they're doing with their own lives, let alone understand what's best for someone else. The biggest regret you'll ever have is not daring to live your life on your own terms. To quote the 18/40/60 rule by psychiatrist Dr Daniel Amen: 'When you're 18, you worry about what everybody's thinking of you. When you're 40, you don't give a damn what anybody thinks about you. And when you're 60, you realize nobody's been thinking about you at all.'

- **THE PATTERN:** You apologize even when you're not in the wrong because you're perpetually scared of offending people and ending up alone.

  THE PATH FORWARD: Ask yourself, 'Did I really do something wrong or am I just people pleasing again?' Apologize only when you're in the wrong. If you need to accept mistakes you didn't even make to stop someone from leaving your life, it's better to live without them. You deserve all the love in the world, and if a set of people can't offer it to you doesn't mean it won't find you eventually.

- **THE PATTERN:** You don't ask for help because you think nobody cares about you.

  THE PATH FORWARD: Some people love you so much that they keep you in their prayers. They want you to grow in life. Be grateful for them. Please know that asking for help is one of the bravest things you can do. Don't feel guilty for it. Your friends share their problems with you, and you're allowed to do the same, unapologetically.

Here's the thing—it takes self-awareness and courage to accept that sometimes, you are the one destroying your peace by allowing problematic behaviour to stem from yourself and accepting the same from others. But the good news is, you can change everything for the better, one day at a time. You owe it to yourself to make space for love and warmth in your life and discard everything that makes you question your worth. I'm sending hugs your way.

18

RE-PARENTING, BECAUSE WHY NOT?

My sister, three years older than I, has always been an overachiever. She'd score the perfect grades in school, participate in debates and extempore and is now a doctor. We went to the same school till I was in the seventh grade. It was a really toxic space. I wasn't good at academics back then, and I still remember how they'd keep comparing me to her. In school, a teacher made me stand in front of everybody and said, 'You know your total marks in all the subjects are still less than what your sister has scored in a single subject.' The entire class laughed. I can still hear the laughter in my ears. Every teacher would remind me that I wasn't good enough. They'd praise my sister in my class only to ridicule me and make me feel bad about myself. They made me feel stupid every day, to the point where I lost all motivation to go to school. My relatives would keep admiring my sister. My parents always motivated me to study harder, but the more people compared me to her, the worse I felt about myself. In that entire chaos, my sister was the only one who saw potential in me. She told me I didn't have to feel bad for not scoring well. She reminded me that I was still young, and it didn't really matter how well or how less I scored.

My mother got transferred to another city when I was in the eighth grade, and this time, she decided to put me and my sister in two different schools. There, I found a teacher who restored my faith in myself by believing in me. Jyothi Williams ma'am was my English teacher in the eighth grade. She was the first one who recognized that I had a command over the English language. Four months in the new school, she started sending me to all the competitions—debates and extempore to begin with. I started anchoring for all the major school events. Her faith in me motivated me so much that I started studying. For the first time in my life, teachers were seeing me for myself and not as my sister's underachieving brother. They saw potential in me, and I couldn't prove them wrong. I never scored less ever again. I was topping every class, every year.

The point of the story is that there are so many people who hurt us when we're young, and there's not much we're able to do about it as children. A relative can comment on your appearance, and that can stay with you forever. A teacher can make you feel like you're not good enough. Your parents can hit you or say something so hurtful that you simply can't seem to get over it. We carry all the trauma into adulthood, and it impacts our lives every day.

For the major part of my life, I was scared of becoming the seventh-grade Rithvik again—the laughing stock. I tortured myself into scoring well. I had to be an overachiever because I tied my entire self-worth to it, thanks to the toxic teachers I had to deal with. Here's what I realized—the seventh-grade Rithvik is always with me. I can feel his presence in my anxious thoughts whenever I don't feel good enough. I started viewing that version of myself as an individual who lives within me. The world wasn't kind to him, and so, I ensure every day that I'm kind to him. That I don't let him feel like he's not good enough. That I remind him that just because he was stuck in a toxic environment doesn't mean he deserved it. That he did achieve everything he wanted to achieve, and even if he hadn't, he'd still deserve all the love of the world.

You must've been hurt as a child, too. You must also be carrying unpleasant voices in your heart that refuse to leave. When you start believing that there's a child within you who deserves your love, you start being kinder to yourself. When you realize that every time you remind that child that he deserves love, you're healing a part of yourself.

Here's how you can be gentle with your inner child/younger self:

1. Think of a traumatic childhood experience that still affects you. Write a letter to your younger self explaining how it wasn't their fault that it happened. That they were young and didn't deserve it. That you're sorry they had to go through that, and you're here to take care of them. That things did get better eventually. That you'll always ensure they feel the safety they deserve.
2. When someone hurts you, talk to yourself with compassion. Every time you curse or belittle yourself, you make your inner child feel unsafe. You need to be there for your inner child. You need to display kindness towards yourself as much as possible.

3. Allow yourself to cry when something triggers you or makes you anxious. Pent-up feelings are future dormant anxiety.
4. Don't be with people who make you feel unsafe. People who trigger your past trauma. People who make you feel unworthy of love.
5. Stay close to the people who love you so much that your inner child feels safe around them. When you can laugh like a child around them, make innumerable memories and speak your heart out—all without worrying if the person is going to hurt you or leave your life eventually.
6. The seventh-grade Rithvik craved for supportive teachers and empathetic relatives. He couldn't find them. But I can be supportive and empathetic towards him now. I can always choose to stay gentle with my heart.
7. Don't be scared of seeking therapy. It'll change your entire life if you find a good therapist.

8. What were the hobbies you had as a child but gave up eventually, thanks to capitalism? Practice them again. Reintroduce your inner child to them.
9. Visualize holding your younger self's hand and remind them that you're here now, and they're safe. Remind them that you won't allow anyone to hurt them going forward.
10. Allow yourself to be loved. Remind yourself that you deserve love in its softest, warmest form, and when it comes to you, don't push it away.

Being in touch with your inner child will change your life completely. Because every time you'll catch yourself being unkind or harsh to yourself, you'll remember that there's a younger self who kept yearning for love, and they deserve only love—boundless, overflowing and unconditional love.

If you found this book helpful, please write to @wordsofrithvik on Instagram. He'd love to hear from you!

REFERENCES

Claude M. Steele, 'The Psychology of Self-Affirmation: Sustaining the Integrity of the Self', *Advances in Experimental Social Psychology* 21 (1988), https://doi.org/10.1016/S0065-2601(08)60229-4

Jamie Waters, 'Constant Craving: How Digital Media Turned Us All Into Dopamine Addicts', *Guardian*, 22 August 2021, https://www.pressreader.com/usa/the-guardian-usa/20210823/281861531588557

Julianne Holt-Lunstad, Timothy B. Smith and J. Bradley Layton, 'Social relationships and mortality risk: a meta-analytic review', *PLoS Med* 7, no. 7 (27 July 2010), https://pubmed.ncbi.nlm.nih.gov/20668659/

Kendra Cherry, 'The Importance of Maintaining Structure and Routine During Stressful Times', Verywell Mind, updated 14 April 2025, https://www.verywellmind.com/the-importance-of-keeping-a-routine-during-stressful-times-4802638

Özlem Adyuk and Ethan Kross, 'From a distance: Implications of spontaneous self-distancing for adaptive self-reflection', *Journal of Personality and Social Psychology* 98, no. 5 (2010), https://doi.org/10.1037/a0019205

Stephen R. Covey, *The 7 Habits of Highly Effective People* (USA: Free Press, 1989)

'Tackling Your Worries', NHS, https://www.nhs.uk/every-mind-matters/mental-wellbeing-tips/self-help-cbt-techniques/tackling-your-worries/

Tracy Swartz, 'I'm a psychiatrist — here's an easy way to stop being a people pleaser',

New York Post, 15 July 2024, https://nypost.com/2024/07/15/health/psychiatrist-reveals-easy-way-to-stop-being-a-people-pleaser/

THE END

Scan QR code to access the
Penguin Random House India website